The Complete Guide to Writing, Editing, Designing, and Self-Publishing Your Books

ROOK COMMUNICATIONS

ISBN 10: 0-9766653-8-7
ISBN 13: 978-0-9766653-8-0

Publisher Information:
Rook Communications
P.O. Box 571
Manassas, VA 20108

Email: vic@victorrook.com

Website:
Go to victorrook.com to order books and DVDs

Interior and Cover Design: Victor Rook

TABLE OF CONTENTS

INTRODUCTION

Why Self-Publish?

You are in control. That is the #1 reason writers choose to self-publish. You don't need a publisher or agent to decide if what you have to say is important. You have final word on how your cover looks, and all the words inside. You also have full say on how your book is distributed and marketed. Plus you retain all rights to your published material. But to get to the point of self-publishing, you must check your ego.

I have worked with many first-time authors who were hoping that a publisher would immediately snatch up their books and make them *New York Times* Best Sellers. So I waited for them to receive their rejection letters, some over several months. They eventually came back to me to help them self-publish. And they couldn't be happier with the results, *and* the instant feedback they got from those who purchased their books.

The reality is, very few books are picked up by major publishers. Those publishers are looking for someone who already has a large following, or a proven track record of successfully selling books. Unless you've committed a major newsworthy crime, are a Hollywood-type with a scandal story, or appear on CNN regularly as a political pundit, chances are you won't be hearing from the Big Five.

Beware of Vanity Publishers

There are a ton of smaller publishing houses that will be more than happy to take your money and print your book. But keep this in mind: No *real* publisher will charge you a penny to publish your book. What these vanity publishers are doing is basically self-publishing your book under their umbrella name, and taking a cut from you. They farm out the formatting and book design and editing to people like me, then give *you* a large bill. I've heard from authors charged in excess of $2000-$3000 per book. That's ridiculous. Some vanity publishers won't charge as much, but they will still take a large cut and maintain control over your book. They'll even make you buy your own book copies from them to sell on your own. And for the most part, you'll still have to do book signings and get the word out on your own. There is limited marketing with these vanity publishers, and much of it you can do on your own.

It might boost your ego to say you have a "publisher," but it is more than likely going to cost you in the long run. Don't be fooled, and don't be a fool. Keep your ego in check. Most readers don't really care who published your book; they care more about the content. And remember, as a self-publisher, you can come up with any name as your own publishing imprint. You can be Emma Smith Publishing if you want. I'll talk about that later in the book.

Book Design Services

Do you have time to design your own book, or would you rather just keep writing and hand that work over to someone else? This is where I come in. I help other authors *self*-publish their books by designing their covers to their specifications, formatting the interiors for print and Kindle, and publishing their books on their *own* Amazon accounts. I don't want a cut of their profits, I don't want any ownership of their books, and they are free to work with Amazon's KDP (Kindle Direct Publishing) interface to price and sell their own books as they please. I've just made them look pretty.

Again, be wary of book design service companies that also act as vanity publishers. Know the difference. It's best to stick with an independent designer, like me, who can do it for you. My email is vic@victorrook.com. Let me help.

Keeping it Simple

And this brings me to the purpose of this book. If you decide you want to take it all on—be both the writer and designer of your books—then this guide will provide you with step-by-step instructions to do just that. And I am all about simplicity. Mind you, it does take some work…*a lot* of work to get it all right. But it's a process that I've repeated many, many times for other authors.

That's why I stick with easy programs. I design both book covers and interiors using Microsoft Word and PowerPoint. For image manipulation and layering, I use Paint Shop Pro. Why don't I use Photoshop or Adobe Illustrator, or other more common design programs? Two reasons: cost and compatibility.

Microsoft Word

Most everyone has a copy of Microsoft Word on his or her computer. This book includes instructions using Word 2016, which is very similar to the newer versions. If you have another program of choice, chances are you'll be able to follow along just fine. Most writing programs have bold, italic, font selection, paragraph formatting, and header and footer features. You just need to familiarize yourself with how to get to those menus and commands to perform the same tasks outlined in the following pages. I'll briefly cover a few other writing tools at the end of the book.

Microsoft PowerPoint

I have used Adobe Illustrator in the past to lay out all sorts of artwork. I also know that when I deliver a product to a customer, they may not have that program. But most likely they will have PowerPoint as part of their MS-Office suite. In this book I will be using PowerPoint for easy cover layout. This allows my clients to open the files I give them and make changes in the future on their own if they want. Just make sure you save the files with embedded fonts.

Paint Shop Pro

Years ago I wanted to design my own book. Reason being, I didn't have the money to have someone else do it. But Photoshop and other programs were way too expensive. Still are. Paint Shop Pro is a program similar to Photoshop that costs a fraction of that. I think it's still under $100. At one time it was free shareware.

So if I need to manipulate photos, like layer images, Paint Shop Pro is my go-to application. But if you'd rather use Photoshop, go right ahead. I will talk about typical image manipulation for book covers within this book.

PDF Programs

The last program you will need is a pdf generator. If you can't afford Adobe Acrobat PDF Creator, I suggest using PDF Complete (pdfcomplete.com) for book interior and PDF Creator (pdfforge.org) for covers. These programs allow you to produce print-quality PDFs from your Word and PowerPoint files. These are the files you will be submitting to Amazon's KDP for your print book. For Kindle, you can submit in Word or html. More on that in the following chapters.

Getting Started

So at this point I take it you have written your book in some program and are now looking for formatting and cover design assistance. But before you do that, please check out the next few chapters to learn how you can best set up your writing program to make the tasks of writing and editing a bit easier down the line.

Are you ready? Let's get started!

WRITING YOUR BOOK

The Basics

You have MS-Word open and a blank page in front of you. Hopefully you've written a short outline of your book by now. If you haven't, go do that. Now change your default Normal font to Times New Roman 12 pt. To do this, go to the Home tab and right-click on the Normal style. Then select Modify. Make the change as below.

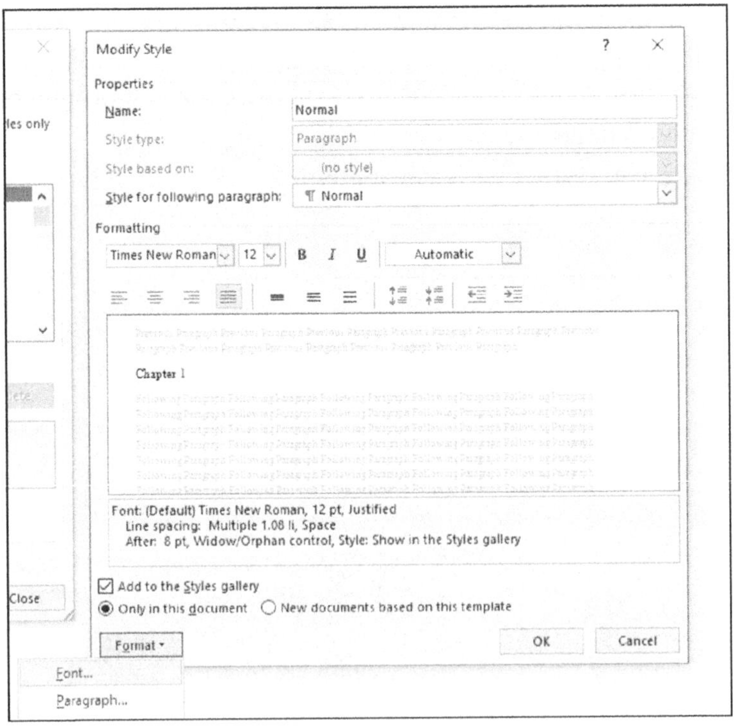

Normal is the text style for most of your book. Other styles include Heading 1, 2, 3, etc. We can alter the font of those later when formatting, but this is a great start.

Next, click on the Format drop-down box at the bottom and choose Paragraph. Choose Justified under Alignment, and .25" First line under Special. I don't recommend having body paragraphs indented more than that. You can later use only Left and Right indents to set off special passages, like written letters, etc.

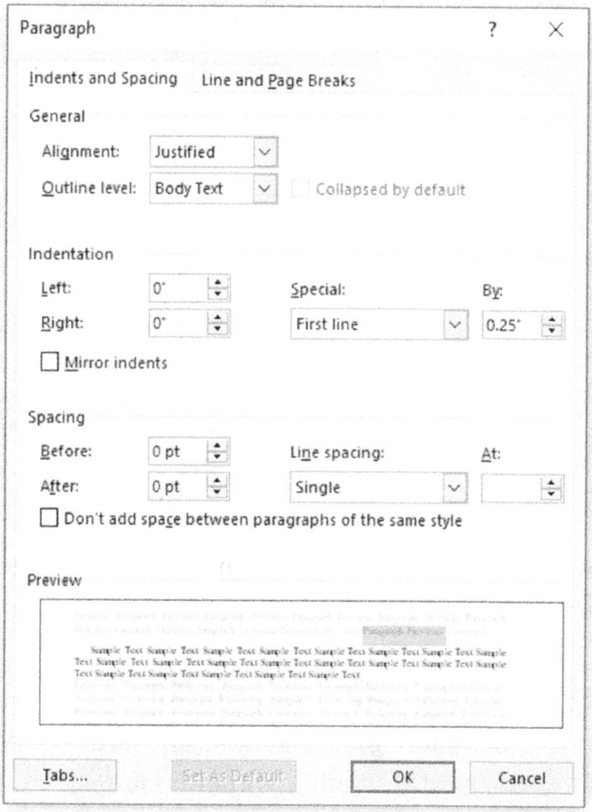

Now when you type, each new paragraph will automatically indent .25" after you hit a return. And the text will be flush on both left and right, which is how books are professionally formatted. Some paragraphs, like the first paragraph in a chapter or after a heading, you will not want indented. We'll talk more about paragraph formatting and tables in the Formatting Your Book chapter.

Next, set View to Print Layout and zoom percentage to Page Width so you can easily read what you type. Seeing words larger on the screen makes them seem more important. Plus it's easier to correct mistakes.

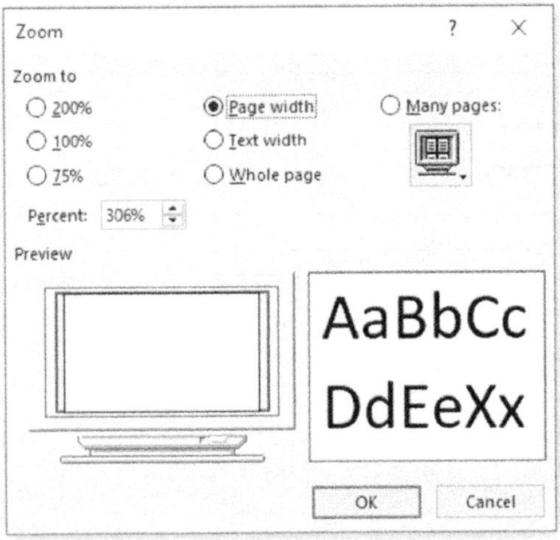

Now begin writing. All you want to do now is get your story out. Let it flow without worry.

Initial Formatting and Punctuation

As you type, definitely **bold** and *italicize* words that you see fit. Bold is not used that often within book text, except for heading styles. Italics are used for *emphasizing* a word.

Refrain from typing in ALL CAPS TO EMPHASIZE. The only time you should use all caps in book text is, for instance, if you are describing a sign. "He took one look at the DEAD END sign and decided to turn back."

When you come to a new chapter, separate out the title by making it bold if you want. We'll work on formatting those chapter headings in the Formatting Your Book section.

Avoid These Common Mistakes

I'm just going to list these because they will cause you problems later during formatting:

1. Never use the Tab key to indent. Use Paragraph formatting or Tables. I will get to that in the Formatting Your Book chapter.
2. Never use your space bar to move text. No book should have two spaces in a row. The first thing I do when formatting a book is remove all double spaces. There is no need for two spaces anywhere.
3. Do not type two spaces after a period. This is a habit learned back in typewriter days. MS-Word and most other programs automatically add a space and a half after each period.
4. Never use the Return key to move to another page. Insert a Page Break within a chapter, or a Section Break to break between chapters. The last thing you want in a book, especially an ebook, is a ton of paragraph returns to remove.
5. Stick with one color. Write in black. You can alter colors later if you intend on printing a book with interior color.

Note Takers

It's inevitable that your best ideas will come when you are nowhere near a computer or your preferred writing tools. You could be barreling down the interstate when the title for a future book, a new plot twist on a current one, or an entire awesome sentence comes to mind. And if you're like me, it will quickly fade away like the detailed nuances of a morning dream.

The solution is simple: Get a voice recorder. These have to be the handiest tools for anyone who wants to capture the muse before she goes on the lam. Sure most smartphones have apps with voice recording capabilities, but in the time that it takes to fire up that app, your brain synapses could misfire and alter your original awesome thoughts. Split-second timing is essential.

I personally use two Olympus voice recorders that I purchased years ago. I keep one in the car, and one on my bed stand. Many of my ideas come while I'm driving, and I am definitely not one to take my eyes off the road with a cell phone. So I have one recorder neatly tucked into the center coin tray of my Hyundai Santa Fe. It takes less than two seconds for me to reach down, press record, and transform my brilliant ideas into ones and zeros. Other ideas come while I'm resting, so one in the house near my bed or within easy reach anywhere inside helps out.

The best part about these digital note takers is that they store each recording separately. The counters show you how many notes you have so you can forward through and review them later. Some allow you to download the recordings to your computer as separate audio files via a USB connection. But I prefer to just review them on the recorder at a later date and delete each one once the task, or idea, has been taken care of. Why make more work?

I've also found these recorders handy to just record what I'm thinking. For instance, for my book *In Search of Good Times*, I recorded a few minutes of me talking through the plot points of the book and what the main character might go through on his journey across the country. It's thinking out loud while recording at the same time. Listening to it play back helped me keep the focus of the book to my original passionate idea. It's like digital therapy—and free.

Name Generators

What's in a name? A lot. Trying to come up with character names that fit their personalities can be quite a task. Plus you'll be typing those names over and over again, so you better like how they sound. I like to choose names that are easy to pronounce, but that's just my prerogative.

Luckily, there are apps and websites that can help. Check out Name Generator (https://www.name-generator.org.uk/) and Writer's Den (http://writers-den.pantomimepony.co.uk/) for a good selection. Also search your smartphone app stores for Name Generators.

Male name - Ardal Kelly
Female name - Jessica Kelly
Male name - Raine Moreau
Female name - Lucille Moreau

Just Write

This is the fun part of making a book. It's where you let all your ideas flow. It's always good to review some basic grammar and punctuation books before putting your words to screen so you have less to edit afterward. I like to do a quick edit after I've written a few paragraphs or so. I reread what I've written above to get myself back into the flow. And if I catch a mistake, I nip it in the bud.

But this is the time to let your ship sail. If it's a fiction book, you probably have an idea of how your story should begin and end. And you probably have figured out some of the high points in the middle. If you are creating a non-fiction book, you've probably done some research to formulate your ideas and written a basic outline.

The point is to enjoy what you're writing and never hold back. Be free with your expression. Don't worry about what other people will think if you're writing a book with a mass murderer. Or one with sexually suggestive scenes. Or if you have a strong opinion on politics you'd like to share. Books are meant to entertain, inform, and teach.

When you write, change up locations now and then. I get tired of typing at my desktop computer. Often times I will sit in my car with the sun shining through the windows and compose my thoughts on a portable writing device. Being outdoors frees up my mind. You might enjoy writing in a coffee shop. A lot of people do. It can be inspiring. Observe people—what they wear, how they move, how they talk—and develop character traits for your fiction work.

Another helpful tool is a simple timer. Force yourself to remain writing for at least an hour. This could be outlining future chapters, developing characters, researching facts, etc. I put together a little writing kit from Dollar Tree items. It consists of an egg timer, a journal, a stylus/pen, and a carrying case for the journal or a tablet. But the timer is most important. It will force you to remain thinking about your book, even if the ideas aren't rushing all at once. You must dedicate yourself to spending time nurturing your craft, even if few words are written. It's not always what's on the page; sometimes it's just getting your mind to feel out your story.

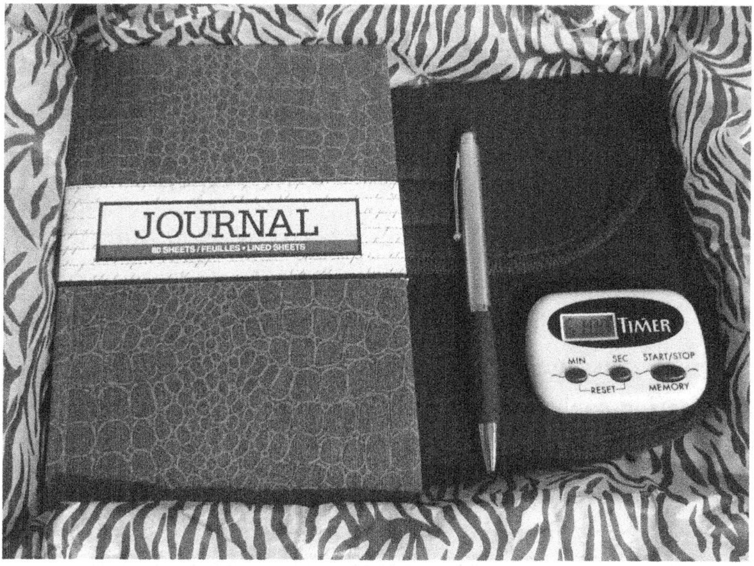

Your First Book

My first book, *Musings of a Dysfunctional Life*, was a memoir of sorts consisting of a series of short stories. Each little musing was no more than 3-4 pages. I liked the idea of putting to words minute memories in a funny or poignant way. And I could pump out one story every few days.

Many first-time authors will choose a project that may not have an end in sight for years—like an epic novel. If that's your choice, be prepared for some kick-ass staying power. Can you see yourself working on the same book for a year or two or three? I spent three years writing *In Search of*

Good Times. I did give myself a four-month break, but I had the gumption to see it through to its completion. Though the *Musings* book was equally as long, it was composed of "bits" or completed stories where each was a separate and complete unit unto itself. This gave me the satisfaction of finishing something—over and over again. Does that make sense?

On the contrary, a novel is always open-ended. It's always unfinished business. A children's book with detailed illustrations can take many months as well. And the cost of hiring an illustrator may be more than you'd want to spend on your initial book.

My suggestion is to write a book of short stories first. This will hone your craft immensely. Each new story will have to have different characters, different plot twists, different messages, etc. And you will feel a great sense of satisfaction each time you complete a short story. Soon you'll have an entire book ready to edit and format.

So now I must leave you for that long journey. Set your sail and soar! In a few months, or even years, I'll see you back here on the other side when you are ready to progress to the next chapter: Editing Your Book.

EDITING YOUR BOOK

Welcome Back

I see you're back already. Is your book finished? Or are you just jumping ahead? That's okay. I get it. You want all the knowledge up front so you can make some wise decisions when it comes to perfecting your book. I don't blame you. Just like making a film, editing shapes your story. It's all in the editing, they say. So let's get started.

Editing Your Own Book

You will often hear, and it's true, that you need more than one pair of eyes to find all the mistakes. And that's great if you have a family member or friend who wants to read your rough drafts. And I highly recommend that you let a few people in on that. If you can't afford to hire a professional editor, there are some things you can do on your own to catch more mistakes. Editing takes time, though. This is not a weekend thing. Editing can take months. But it will be worth it in the end. So…let's get started!

Content vs. Line Editing

Content editing is manipulating your story so it works well. Finessing the plot, enriching the characters, being more descriptive are some of the ways you edit the content. Does it have a grabber opening? Does it build to crescendo? Will the ending blow people away? If it's a non-fiction book, do you have all the components in the book that you need? Is all the research there? Do you have your facts straight?

Line editing is what you will do *after* you've edited for content. You will check for tense, point-of-view, and any inconsistencies. You should also check for spelling, grammar, punctuation, and overuse of words. I once had an author incorporate three versions of the word look (looked, looking, look) in the same sentence. That is almost a feat in itself. I convinced him to use more descriptive words, like stared, glared, squinted, or gazed throughout his book.

Content Editing is beyond the scope of this book. Only you will know if your story works or if your book is finished. But you can get others' input as well. After you turn your rough draft into a less-rough draft (draft 2), that is when you should let other people in. But remember, everyone has an opinion. That's the catch-22. When you tell someone to look for mistakes, that can take them away from the story. So ask them before you hand over your manuscript if the story works and if they understand what's going on. They may catch some grammatical, spelling, and punctuation errors along the way, but what you're really looking for is their overall feeling about what you've written.

Once you've made any necessary changes to make the story work, let others reread it. You will know when it's done and if you've covered all the bases. Your opinion is the one that matters most. Are *you* satisfied with the results? If so, then it's time to move on to Line Editing.

Spelling and Grammar

Most writing programs have spelling and grammar check, but use these features with a bit of caution. They can sometimes suggest an incorrect change. Like this.

As you type in MS-Word, a squiggly line will appear under problem words and sentences. But it won't catch everything. It might not detect the difference between "maybe" and "may be," for instance. So instead of correcting at your own risk based on the program's suggestions, look up grammar rules and spelling on the internet. For spelling, check with dictionary.com. Take free grammar quizzes on grammarbook.com and grammar-monster.com. They're an excellent way to strengthen your grammar skills. I suggest these books as well: *The Blue Book of Grammar and Punctuation*, *The Elements of Style*, *Line by Line: How to Edit Your Own Writing*, *Painless Grammar (Barron's Painless Series)*, and *Eats, Shoots & Leaves: The Zero Tolerance Approach to Punctuation.*

Punctuation

Punctuation is key to helping your reader comprehend what you are trying to convey to them in your story or book. The most common punctuation mistakes I see are with commas, quotes, and hyphens (and em dashes). Let's explore each.

Commas

Commas are your friends. So treat them properly. Don't overuse or underuse commas. In dialogue, you need commas to separate the speaker from what he or she says.

> *He turned to me and said, "It's okay if you want to go to the prom with someone else."*

> *"I don't want to go to the store," he said.*

Commas also separate clauses in a sentence.

> *Before she could answer, her friend walked in to break up the tension.*

Notice how both clauses have a noun and a verb.

Commas also separate conjunctive adverbs:

> *Apparently, he never took that into consideration.*

> *He never said he was sorry, however.*

Commas also separate items in a list.

> *The only people invited were Sally, John, and Roger.*

Note: Grammar Nazis have fought for years over the last comma, also known as the Oxford comma. The argument is that the word "and" suffices enough. This is the rule as I know it. For novels and fiction books, include the comma. For AP-style work, like articles and news stories, remove the last comma.

Quotation Marks

Quotation marks, both single and double, can be used in a variety of ways. Mostly you will see them used in dialogue:

> *"I said to her, 'look at that dress. Isn't it lovely?'"*

Now, I purposely chose to use one example sentence for quotation marks. It covers all the bases. First, you put double quotes around the entire sentence because it is one person speaking. Second, I put single quotes around the portion of the sentence where the woman states what she said to another person. And lastly, I did not put any other punctuation marks (like a period) at the end of the sentence because the ? and quotes suffice.

When writing dialogue, you start a new paragraph for each person speaking. Once it's established who is speaking, you don't need to add the person's name each time.

> *"I like working out on Friday nights," Tom said.*
> *"Me too," Jim replied.*
> *"The gym seems to be a lot less crowded then."*
> *"Yeah, and it helps me concentrate better."*

It's understood who is talking in the last two sentences. If you have a lot of back-and-forth dialogue, you can add some sort of notification to remind readers who is at the helm.

> *"Yeah, and it helps me concentrate better."*
> *Tom set down the 50-lb dumbbell. "You got that right."*

Hyphens & Em Dashes

I see many misuses of these two very important punctuation marks. So let's get down to what they do.

A hyphen (-) is created by pressing the key to the right of 0 (zero) on your keyboard. It is short and used for combining words. For example:

> *The well-made dress displayed in the department store.*

If the sentence were rewritten without well-made as an adjective to dress, you would not include the hyphen.

> *The dress displayed in the department store is well made.*

Other uses include separating numbers.

> *The ratio of people to cars was 8-1.*

An em dash (—) is like a longer hyphen, and it is created in MS-Word by pressing Ctrl-Alt and the minus sign on your keyboard's numerical keypad (on the right). Do not get in the habit of putting two hyphens next to each other like -- in place of an em dash.

Em dashes separate statements within a sentence that you want to set apart. In other words, those statements can be removed without changing the true meaning of the sentence.

> *It was the last time she went to the store—the one located on Green Ave. and P Street—before she left town.*

You can also use an em dash to set off a statement at the end of a sentence.

> *Roger was a great spiritual leader—one of the best.*

Notice how I did not put any spaces before or after the em dashes. Also, you want to avoid overusing em dashes throughout a book. It can get very tiring to look at.

Colons and Semicolons

Let's get to the point. Use the colon (:) when you are introducing a list, or when leading into further information.

> *These are the basic school subjects: reading, writing, and arithmetic.*

> *In order to achieve the best results, you will want to do the following:*

The semicolon (;) is used within a sentence to separate two independent clauses, meaning what comes after the semicolon has both a subject and a verb, too.

> *He went to the school on Jackson Street; she went to the one on Wyoming.*

These two clauses could easily be divided into two separate sentences, but they are so closely related in thought that a semicolon would also suffice.

Proofing Methods

Once your book has been written and edited for spelling, grammar, and punctuation, you are going to want to proofread the book several times—at least four. Give a copy to a trusted friend who knows something about the aforementioned rules.

One thing I've noticed to help me proof my own books over the years is printing out or viewing the book in a way that is different from what I've seen it while writing. That could mean printing it out on paper with different margins, or viewing it on a tablet. All of a sudden mistakes that I didn't catch while viewing it on a screen pop right out. That's because your eyes get used to seeing it the same way, errors and all.

Proofing is a very tedious job. You'll get sick of reading your own book over and over again. Take a week break if you have to. Once you've received feedback from others, go back into the document and make those corrections. Be careful, though. Sometimes you can introduce other mistakes with corrections. Hence, go through your book several times until you catch them all.

FORMATTING YOUR BOOK

Congratulations! You've finished writing your book. Right? You've made the story *perfect* to your liking. You've found every grammatical, spelling, and punctuation mistake known to man and corrected it. Right? If not, you need to turn around and go back to the last chapter. Final formatting is something you only want to do once your book is *completely* written and proofed. Think of it as putting your words into stone, so to speak. Making them look pretty.

Book Size

If you want print copies available for your book, you need to decide on book dimensions. Here are my recommendations:

Size	Types of Books
“6 x 9”	Standard size for most books, novels.
“5.5” x 8.5”	Slightly smaller for above type books.
5” x 8”	Poetry books and small guides.
8.5” x 8.5”	Illustrated children's books. It's square.
8” x 10”	Children's books, illustrated art books.
8.5” x 11”	Craft books and art books.

Cost for books is only dependent on the number of pages and if you want color or black and white interior. Your book must have at least 24 pages for Amazon to print it. The size of the book does not change the cost. If you choose a larger size for the same content, you'll use up fewer pages. Hence, the cost will be cheaper. But stick to the previous table for appropriate sizes for the different book types.

Page Setup

Now that you've completed your document, Save it as a different file name so you have the original. Select View-Print Layout to show pages. Then go to Layout-Margins and select Custom Margins. Set margin dimensions as Top (.75), Bottom (.75), Left (.75), Right (.5), Gutter (.13), Header (.35), Footer (.35), and Gutter position (Left). Select mirror margins and Apply to Whole Document.

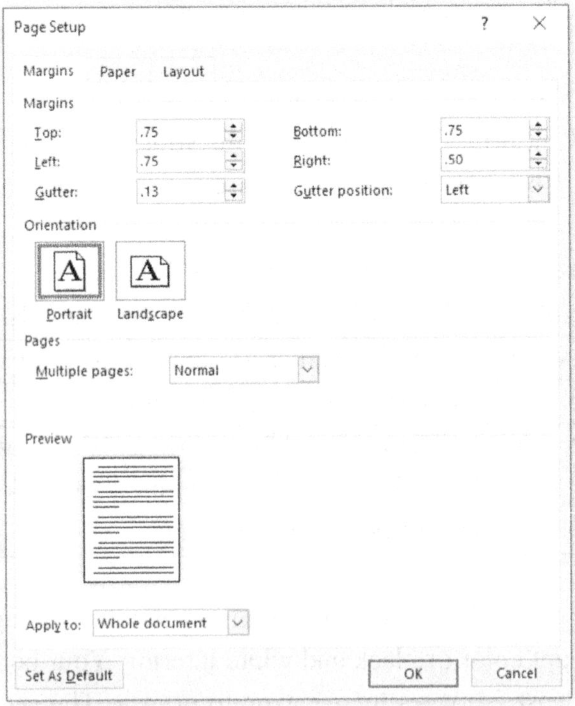

Under the Paper tab, choose your book dimensions and Apply to Whole Document.

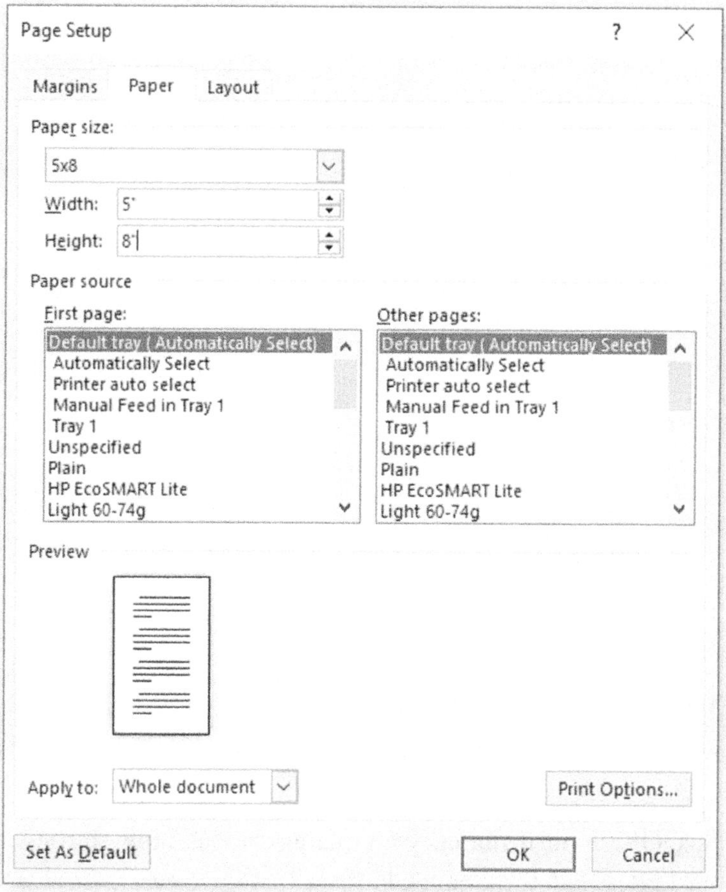

Under the Layout tab, checkmark Different odd and even, Different first page, and Apply to Whole Document.

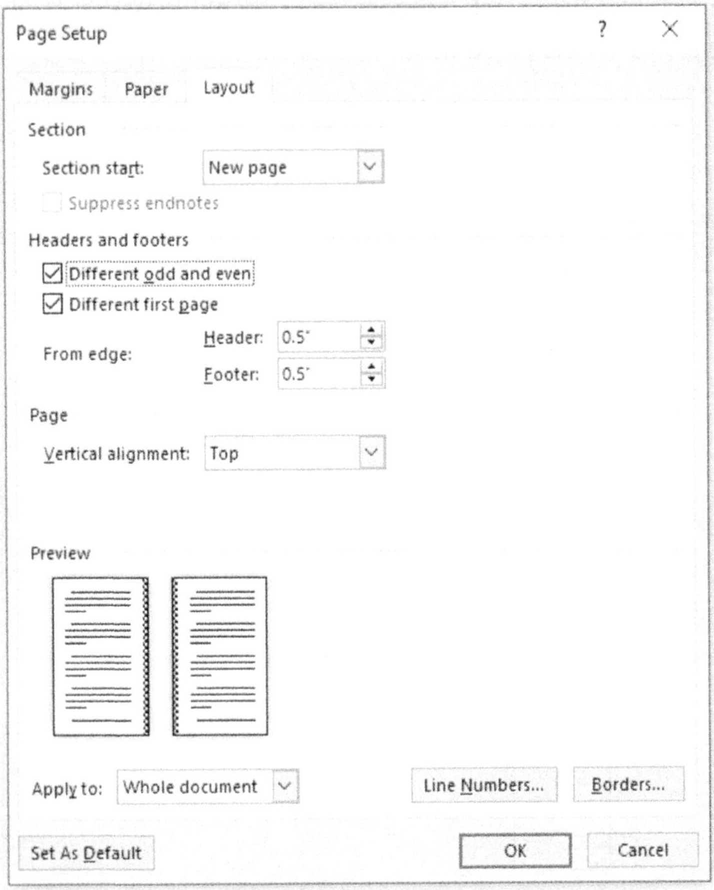

Click OK. You'll notice your manuscript is now starting to look like actual book pages in Print Layout view.

Heading Styles

Heading styles make it easy to format and change the look of your book with little effort. As stated earlier, you will have Styles for the basic text (Normal), and for Headings 1, 2, 3, and so on. I would limit your headings to just three for non-fiction books. One is all you need for novels. That would be the chapter titles.

I'm assuming that you've given each of the chapters in your book a name or number. Right click on every chapter title and choose Heading 1 in the style pop-up. We will alter how it looks later. You just want to make sure you've designated all chapter titles as Heading 1 style.

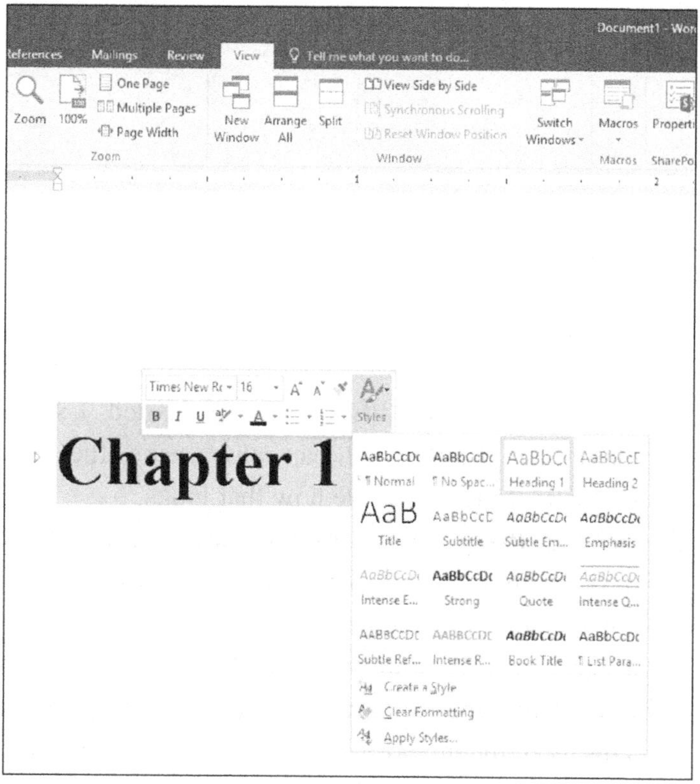

Now you can change the look of the style if desired. Go to the Home tab and right-click on Heading 1. Choose Modify.

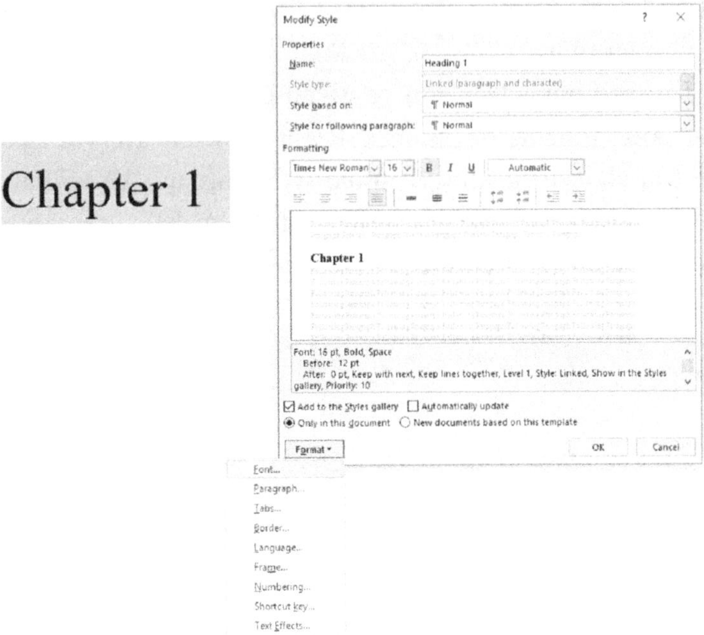

1. Choose Font to modify the font if desired. I suggest making it **Bold**. You can also make the letters UPPERCASE if you like how that looks.
2. Choose Paragraph to center the heading style if desired, and choose the number of points spacing above and below the text. This will allow you to have a gap of space before and after the heading without having to type paragraph returns within your text. This is a much more efficient way of doing so. If you've already placed paragraph returns within the text, you might want to go remove them. It's up to you.

Once you are satisfied with the heading look, choose OK and Apply. Now all chapter titles will match what you've chosen. Play around until you find a style that suits your book.

Repeat this for other headings within your book. You'll want to make subheadings (2, 3, etc.) a little less prominent than the chapter title. In other words, choose a smaller font size or not uppercase, etc. Keep the font size greater than or equal to 12 points, of course. Bold to make it stick out from Normal text.

Fonts

Go to a bookstore and look at other books. See what kinds of fonts are used. Most body text is of a serif typeface, meaning it has jagged edges. They say this makes it easier to read. Chapter headings may be san-serif. Arial is an example of that.

Try to stick with just two font styles for your book interior. Here are some examples of commonly used fonts for printed books:

Serif Fonts	San-serif Fonts
This is Times New Roman	This is Arial
This is Georgia	This is Calibri
This is Garamond	This is Verdana
This is Baskerville	This is Tahoma
This is Palatino	This is Helvetica

You can go a little crazy with title fonts. Just make sure they are readable. These are also good for chapter headings.

This is Cooper BT	*THIS IS ADVENTURE*
This is Comics Sans	*This is Signature*
This is Type-Ra	**This is Impact**
This is Boulder	This is Jokerman

Check out fonts.com for a larger font selection. Also search the web for free fonts. But be wary. Some free font sites may have generic versions of fonts that won't display all characters and punctuation marks correctly.

Later versions of MS-Word also have Design themes with different font typefaces for each of the headings and body text. Access the design themes from the Design tab. Play around and see if you like any. You can always change one or more heading styles as previously discussed.

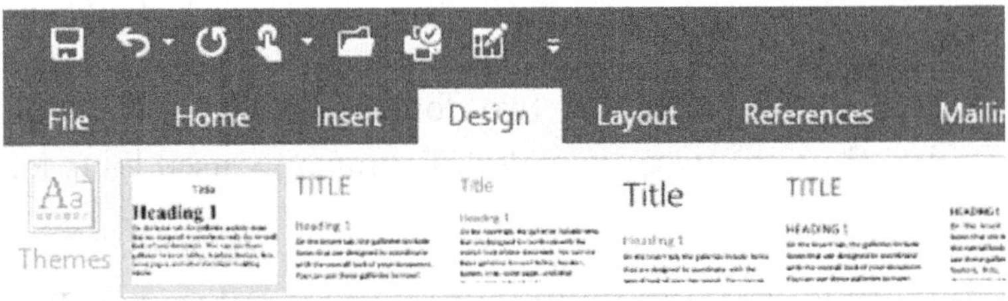

Section Breaks

Most book interiors are broken into sections: title page and copyright page, dedication, table of contents, foreword, introduction, body of book, acknowledgements, etc., in that order. The following is an example of a book with just a title page, copyright page, dedication page, blank page, and body of book. The blank page is created using Layout-Breaks-Page. This is so the first chapter starts on an odd page (right).

In this case it is the fifth page of the book.

What we want to achieve here is that the title page, copyright page, and dedication will not have any page numbers or headers and footers, any intro material will have page numbers like (i,ii,iii, etc.), and the body of the book will have page numbers starting with 1. Section breaks are the only way to achieve this.

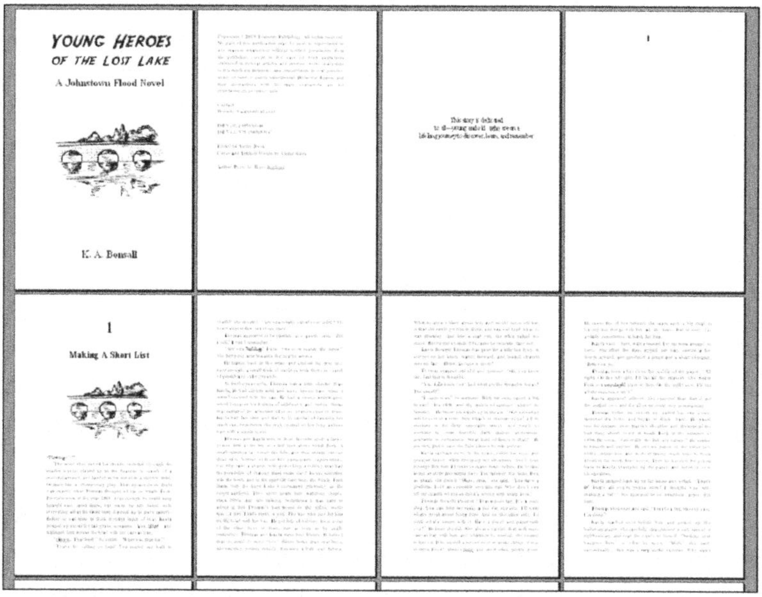

Use a section break, not a page break, to separate those sections. To help you see these breaks, click on the paragraph symbol ¶ on the Home tab. This will show you all paragraph marks, spaces, page breaks, and section breaks. It's like looking into the underbelly of your document. The following image shows a portion of this book with formatting marks displayed.

> One thing I've noticed to help me proof my own books over the years is printing out or viewing the book in a way that is different from what I've seen it while writing. That could mean printing it out on paper with different margins, or viewing it on a tablet. All of a sudden mistakes that I didn't catch while viewing it on a screen pop right out. That's because your eyes get used to seeing it the same way, errors and all.¶
>
> Proofing is a very tedious job. You'll get sick of reading your own book over and over again. Take a week break if you have to. Once you've received feedback from others, go back into the document and make those corrections. Be careful, though. Sometimes you can introduce other mistakes with corrections. Hence, go through your book several times until you catch them all.¶
>
> ¶::::::::::Section Break (Next Page)::::::::::

In the example, we only need to place a section break on the blank page to separate the pages that will not have headers and footers from the pages—the body of the book—that *will* have headers and footers. You will also want to put a section break at the end of each chapter. If we had foreword or introduction sections, they would follow any table of contents and they would need a section break before and after them. There are no headers or footers on a table of contents.

To insert a section break, place your cursor after a paragraph mark at the end of the described sections. Choose Layout-Breaks and click on Section Breaks-Next page.

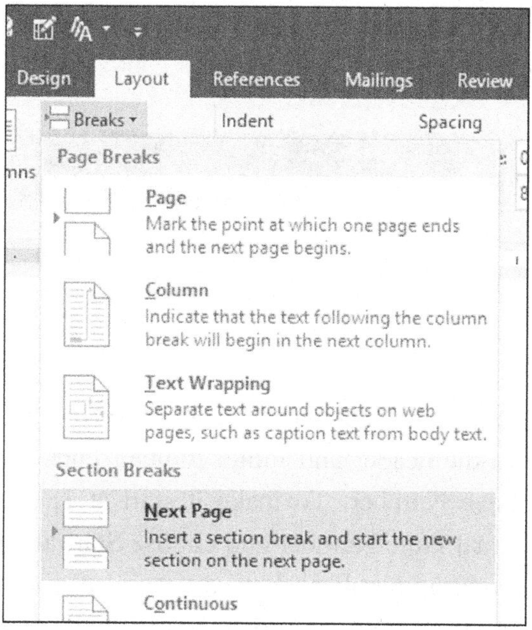

Headers and Footers

Once you have inserted your section breaks, you can now designate your headers and footers. For your headers, you want author name on the left and book title on the right. If your book is short stories, or you want chapter titles in the header, you will want to put the book title on the left (even) pages, and the short story or chapter names on the right (odd) pages. You only want headers and footers on the intro material and body of book. There should be no header on top of the first page of a chapter, however.

To start, place your cursor at the beginning of chapter 1 and click on Insert-Header. Click on Link to Previous to make sure it is toggled off. The words Same as Previous will disappear from the header break. You will want to do this for the first page and the two odd and even pages that follow.

This will keep your headers and footers different from any previous sections.

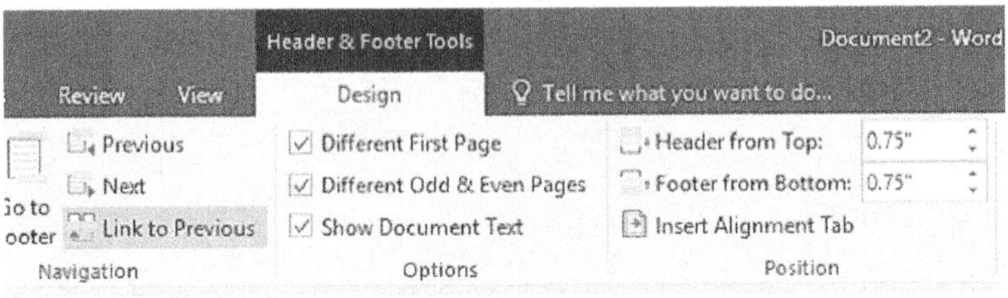

Now place your cursor into the footer of the first page of chapter 1. In the header and footer toolbar, click on the icon for Insert Page Number. To make it start at 1, click on the icon for Format Page Number and choose Start at and type 1. I suggest centering numbers, but you can also make numbers left justified on even pages and right justified on odd pages. Centering is the easiest. Format how you like using the Formatting toolbar. I suggest a font size of 10 pt. bold.

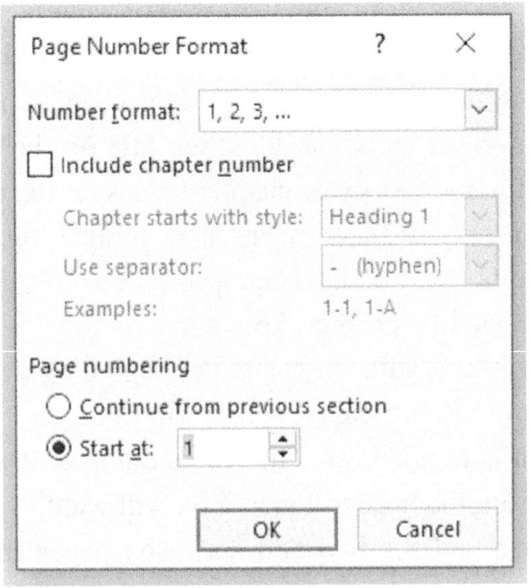

Check to see that all page numbers carry through each chapter. If they don't, put your cursor into the footer section of each chapter and click on Format Page Number. Select Continue from previous section.

For the headers, you want to put your cursor into the header of the second page of chapter 1. You want author name on the left (even) pages, and book title on the right (odd) pages. Make the font 10 pt. bold. You can uppercase the title and author name if you want to further set them off.

Check to see that all headers carry through each chapter, except for the first page of each chapter. If they don't, put your cursor into the headers of each chapter and toggle Same as Previous on from your headers and footers toolbar.

Table of Contents

If you want to have a table of contents for your book, you would put that after the dedication page and blank page so it starts on an odd page. The table of contents comes before any foreword, introduction, or body of book, since you will want those noted in the table of contents.

To automatically generate a table of contents, place your cursor where you want it and choose References-Table of Contents. Select Custom Table of Contents. Check Show page numbers and Right align page numbers if desired.

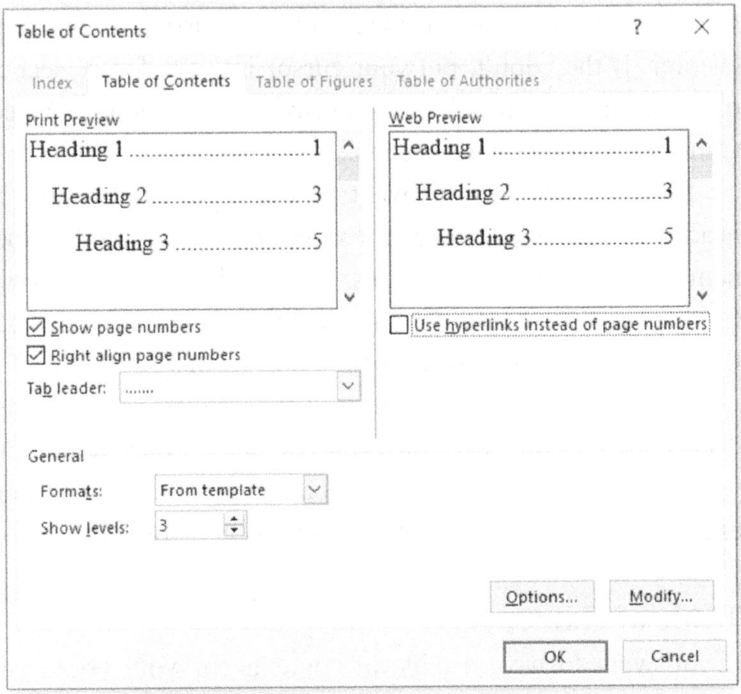

I suggest going with the template format, but you can also play around with the other suggestions. Click OK to automatically generate the table of contents from your heading styles. If you don't like how it looks, delete the table of contents and try again.

Note: Before you print your book, you will want to place your cursor anywhere within the table of contents and right click your mouse. Choose Update Field and select Update entire table. This will make sure all chapter names and page numbers are correct.

Design Ideas

There are many things you can do to spiff up your book interior. For instance, you can insert and repeat a graphic image under the chapter name or number. You can also add a drop cap first letter to the first paragraph of each chapter. Highlight the first letter and choose Insert-Drop Cap. You will need to revert back to no drop cap for Kindle ebook publishing. We'll talk about that later.

4

Mama's Words of Wisdom

"Oh, Kayla, that's ridiculous! He can't mean that!" Kayla's mother responded.

Chapter 5

North African Campaign
Battle of Tunisia

Positioning to Meet the Germans and Italians

Bayer appreciated the fact that his Battalion Surgeon, Captain Hahn, kept his team well briefed on what was likely to take place day to day. Hahn attended regular intelligence briefings and he always shared what he'd learned. Hahn now explained that American and other Allied Forces had wanted to occupy Tunisia quickly to keep it out of the

Tables

You can insert tables into a document to space items into columns and rows if you like using Insert-Table. Again, do not use tabs. You can choose to show grid lines or not. You can also shade rows, etc. Tables can be used for images also.

UNIT	COMMANDER WHILE SERVING
Third Battalion	Lieutenant Colonel Charles T. Homer, Jr
16th Infantry Regiment	Colonels Henry Cheadle and later D'Alary Fechet, George Taylor, Frederick Gibb
1st Infantry Division	Three different Major Generals
V Corps	Four different Major Generals
1st US Army	Three Lieutenant Generals commanding including General Omar Bradley
Medical Detachment of 16th Infantry Regiment	Major Charles Tegtmeyer (Regimental Surgeon after invasion of Sicily)

Inserting Pictures

To insert a picture into your document, place your cursor where you want the picture, click on Insert-Pictures, and choose your image file. You will want to make sure the image is not floating. Right click on the picture and select Picture-Layout and make sure In line with text is selected.

Pictures should be large in pixel size to print well. Use original photos. Once the picture is inserted, you can center it and resize with the corner handles. You can even type a caption underneath it if you want.

Note: If the picture doesn't seem centered, place your cursor on either side of the picture, right click, and choose Paragraph. Remove the .25" First line indent under Special.

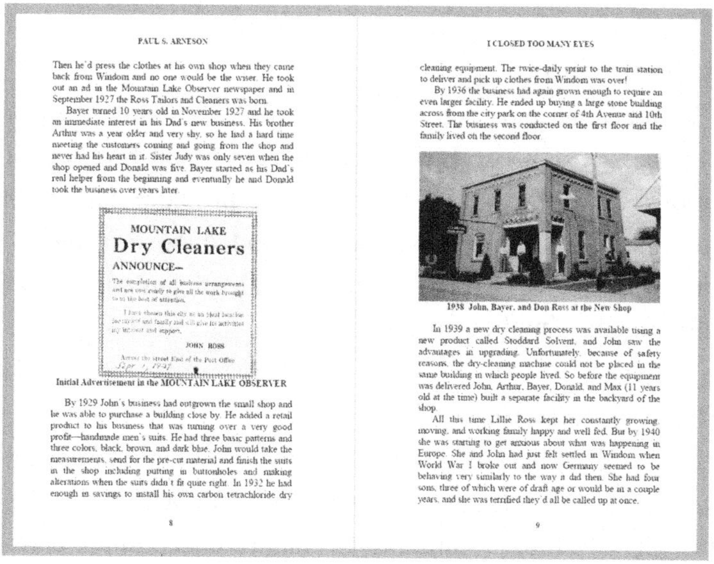

PAUL S. ARNESON

Then he'd press the clothes at his own shop when they came back from Windom and no one would be the wiser. He took out an ad in the Mountain Lake Observer newspaper and in September 1927 the Ross Tailors and Cleaners was born.

Bayer turned 10 years old in November 1927 and he took an immediate interest in his Dad's new business. His brother Arthur was a year older and very shy, so he had a hard time meeting the customers coming and going from the shop and never had his heart in it. Sister Judy was only seven when the shop opened and Donald was five. Bayer started as his Dad's real helper from the beginning and eventually he and Donald took the business over years later.

MOUNTAIN LAKE
Dry Cleaners
ANNOUNCE—
JOHN ROSS
Across the street East of the Post Office

Initial Advertisement in the MOUNTAIN LAKE OBSERVER

By 1929 John's business had outgrown the small shop and he was able to purchase a building close by. He added a retail product to his business that was turning over a very good profit—handmade men's suits. He had three basic patterns and three colors, black, brown, and dark blue. John would take the measurements, send for the pre-cut material and finish the suits in the shop including putting in buttonholes and making alterations when the suits didn't fit quite right. In 1932 he had enough in savings to install his own carbon tetrachloride dry

8

I CLOSED TOO MANY EYES

cleaning equipment. The twice-daily sprint to the train station to deliver and pick up clothes from Windom was over!

By 1936 the business had again grown enough to require an even larger facility. He ended up buying a large stone building across from the city park on the corner of 4th Avenue and 10th Street. The business was conducted on the first floor and the family lived on the second floor.

1938 John, Bayer, and Don Ross at the New Shop

In 1939 a new dry cleaning process was available using a new product called Stoddard Solvent, and John saw the advantages in upgrading. Unfortunately, because of safety reasons, the dry-cleaning machine could not be placed in the same building in which people lived. So before the equipment was delivered John, Arthur, Bayer, Donald, and Max (11 years old at the time) built a separate facility in the backyard of the shop.

All this time Lillie Ross kept her constantly growing, moving, and working family happy and well fed. But by 1940 she was starting to get anxious about what was happening in Europe. She and John had just felt settled in Windom when World War I broke out and now Germany seemed to be behaving very similarly to the way it did then. She had four sons, three of which were of draft age or would be in a couple years, and she was terrified they'd all be called up at once.

9

ISBN Number

You'll need an ISBN number within your print book for it to be available on Amazon. You can buy one or a block of ten at myidentifiers.com (do not purchase barcodes), or you can use a free one that Amazon will provide for you when you set up your book through their KDP platform. Once you get that number, you will put it on your book's copyright page.

ISBN 10: 0-9766653-7-9
ISBN 13: 978-0-9766653-7-3

Hyphenation

To avoid large gaps between words, you can force the book to hyphenate. Choose Layout-Hyphenation and Hyphenation Options. If you just want to hyphenate problem paragraphs, highlight the paragraph beforehand and choose Manual. If you want the entire document hyphenated, choose Automatically hyphenate document.

Final Formatting

In books, the first paragraph of a chapter or section does not have a first-line indent. You will want to place your cursor into all of those paragraphs, right click, and choose Paragraph. Remove the .25" First line indent under Special.

File Cleanup

Select View-Print Layout and under Zoom choose Multiple Pages. Page through your finished book to make sure the headers and footers are correct, the table of contents is updated, and there are no tabs, etc. Bulleted lists are allowed and work well when converted to an ebook.

Create PDF File

Once you are sure everything looks correct, you can print the file as a pdf document. Choose your installed pdf printer under Print and select or enter the correct document size. Make sure you choose 300 dpi and the best quality for print.

Open the pdf file in Adobe Reader and under View-Page Display make sure Two Page View and Show Cover in Two Page View are selected. This will make the book look like left and right pages. The first page will be alone. Use your keyboard Page Up And Page Down keys to move through and check your book.

CHILDREN'S BOOKS

Overview

Illustrated children's books are a different beast to format. Some have pictures that go all the way to the edge, also known as bleed. Some have pictures that stay within the boundaries of the page edges. Those are no-bleed books. You need to decide if your book is bleed or no bleed to set up the dimensions. And in this case, we are going to use PowerPoint to design the book. PowerPoint gives you a lot more flexibility to bring in pictures, move them around, and add text anywhere.

No Bleed

Bleed

Dimensions

If your book has no bleed, the dimensions are the same as the book size. If your book is a bleed book, you will want to add .125" to the width and .25" to the height. This extra space will allow for trimming. Here's an 8" x 10" book example.

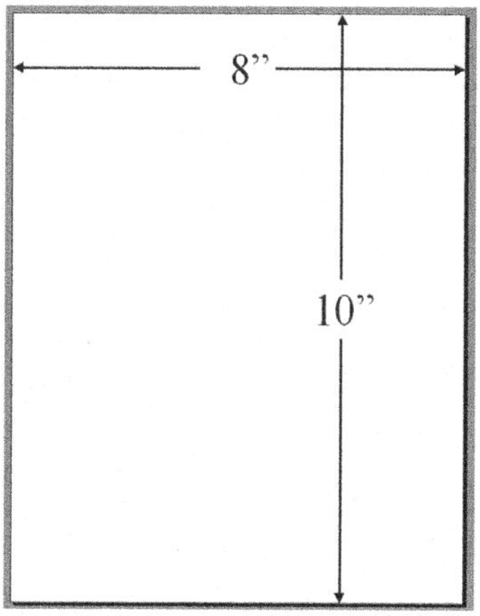

No Bleed

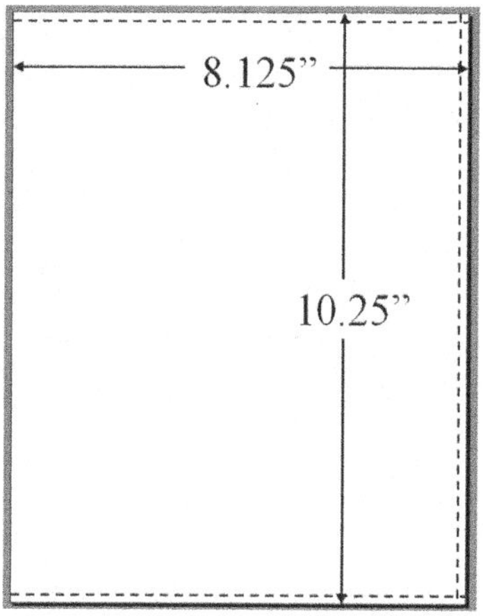

Bleed

Layout

Open PowerPoint and create a blank page. Choose Home-Layout and Blank to make it a blank slide.

Then go to Design-Slide Size-Custom Slide Size and change the dimensions of your book according to those above. Choose Portrait for Orientation.

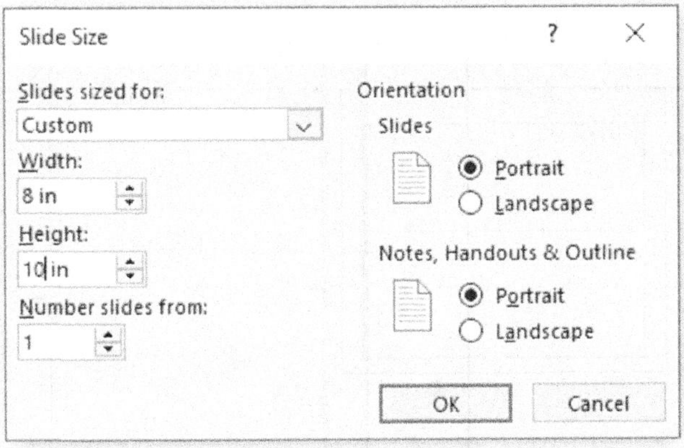

In this case, I will create a no-bleed book. So the dimensions of my page are exactly the book size (8" x 10"). The first page is a right page, which will be bound on the left in a printed book. When you place text and images on each page, you have to shift them to the right a bit on right (odd) pages, and to the left a bit on left (even) pages so they don't get lost in the spine. About .5" will do. You also need to make sure any important text or images are at least .5" from the page edges.

Adding Text & Images

As in any book, the first page is the interior title page. We will add text to the page using the text box icon from the Drawing toolbar under Home. Make a box where you want the text to be and start typing. You can adjust the font and font size afterward, as well as reposition the text box.

Continue to add text with different text boxes. You can also insert images using the Insert-Picture command.

For the rest of the book, you can add more text, images, and even page numbers in the corners. Make sure odd pages numbers are on the right and even are on the left. To insert a new page, choose Insert-New Slide.

Make sure you also include a copyright page, and add blank pages to start the first page on an odd page. Also, add additional pages at the end of the book so the book has an even number of pages.

Note: Your book must have at least 24 pages for Amazon to print it. At any time you can view your entire book by clicking on View-Slide Sorter.

Once your book is finished and proofed, print to pdf. Make sure, again, to enter the correct dimensions of the book, choose 300 dpi, and best quality for print. Open the pdf file in Adobe Reader and under View-Page Display make sure Two Page View and Show Cover in Two Page View are selected. This will make the book look like left and right pages. The first page will be alone. Use your keyboard Page Up And Page Down keys to move through and check your book.

COVER DESIGN

Overview

The old adage "don't judge a book by its cover" shouldn't be taken literally. Because, indeed, the cover of a book is one of its most important selling features. True that it might not accurately represent the quality of the contents, but a poorly designed cover may prevent an otherwise interested reader from checking the book out.

In this section I will talk about three types of book covers: text covers, photo covers, and illustration covers. All will be created using PowerPoint.

Dimensions

With book covers, you have to take into account not only the height and width of the book, but also the spine width. Spine width is determined by the number of pages in the book and the type of paper used. For books printed through Amazon, here's how you calculate spine width:

White interior paper
Spine width = (# pages x .002252")

Color interior paper
Spine width = (# pages x .002347")

You also have to add .125" inch around the entire book dimensions for cutting. Here we will design a book cover that is 5" x 8" with 92 pages printed on regular b&w interior paper.

Book covers are created as full wraparounds, meaning the back, spine, and front are all included onto one page. We will place box guides on the page to show where the book will be cut and bound.

Spine width = (92 x .002252") = .207" or .21"
Overall width = .125" + 5" + .21 + 5" + .125" = 10.46"
Overall height = .125" + 8" + .125" = 8.25"

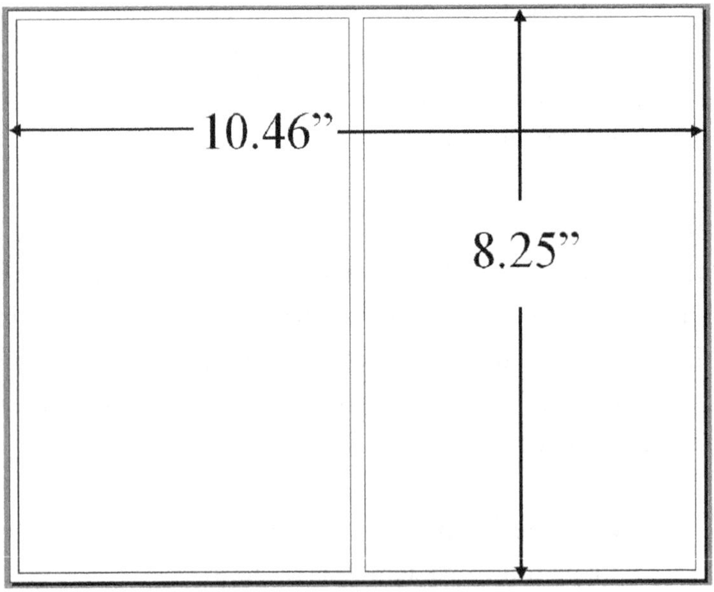

The temporary guide boxes are 5" x 8" and are created using the rectangle icon on the Drawing toolbar under Home. Once you have created the left guide box, position it by right clicking on the edge and selecting Size and Position. Enter

.125" for the horizontal and vertical dimensions from the top-left corner of the page. You can also remove the fill by clicking on the bucket icon in the Format Shape panel.

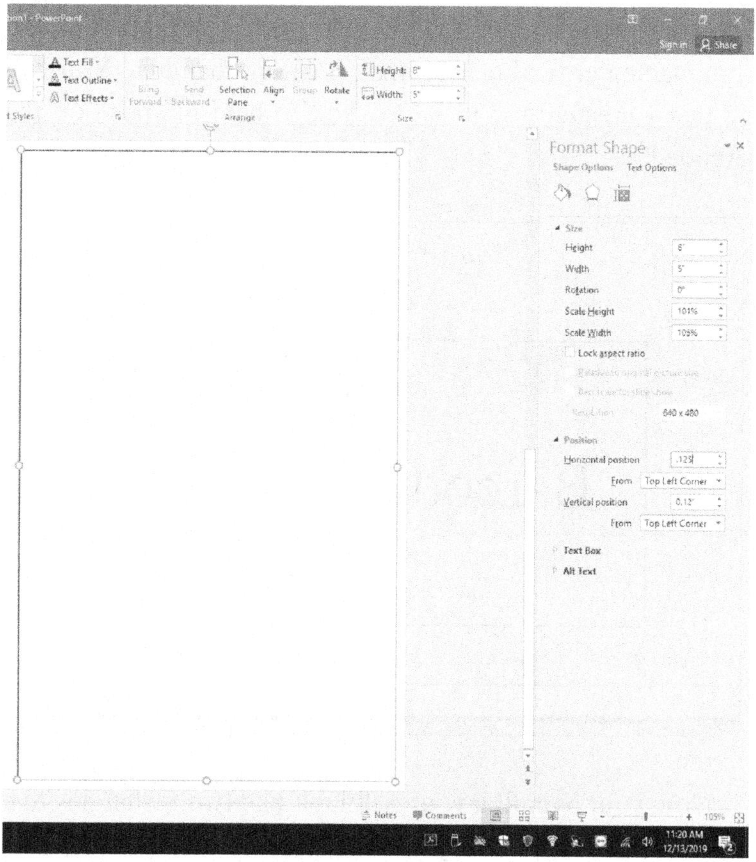

The right box guide will be .125" + 5" + .21" = 5.33" from the top-left corner of the page horizontally, and .125" vertically. Now you know that all text must fit inside the guide boxes and be centered to them if desired.

Now create one more box that is 1.2" high by 2" wide. You can keep it filled white. This will be a guide box to show you where the barcode will be printed on the back cover. We will remove the guide boxes and barcode box prior to creating the final pdf. The barcode box should be positioned .25" from the back bottom guide line and .25" to the left of it. Knowing where the barcode will be printed will prevent you from placing critical text or images within that area. You will see that I created a .25" x .25" box to help me position the barcode box.

Now your overall layout will look like two rectangles that match the dimensions of your book, and a barcode box. From here you will position photos and graphics and text within the boxes. Text can also be added and rotated to fit the spine. If you make changes to your book interior that increases or decreases the page count, you will need to alter the dimensions of your cover. That's why it's best to wait till your book is finished before designing the cover.

Text Covers

Many best-selling books have text-only covers with maybe a few inserted images. Use different font typefaces, colored boxes, and other design elements to give it more oomph.

Photo Covers

Covers using photo backgrounds can really make your book stand out. You can use photos that you've taken, or search for them on royalty-free sites like pixabay.com. It's not required, but it's a good practice to donate to the artist on these sites if you use their photo.

Search for high-resolution photos that have large spans of solid areas so text you place on top of the image will stand out. Here I found a photo that has a lot of sky.

Add the photo to your layout using Insert-Pictures. Then resize and crop the photo to fit the dimensions. To crop, right click on any of the picture handles and select Crop. Then adjust image. Lastly, choose Home-Arrange and Send to Back so it is under the guide boxes. I made the guide box color lighter so the boxes would be more visible.

Now you can add text with different fonts and colors if desired. Notice how I made use of the solid areas here. Spine text can be added if your book is over 120 pages. Make sure the spine text is .0625" away from guides.

I took this cover one step further by creating a composite background in Paint Shop Pro. I took the original photo and added a map to the sky and a compass using Layers. I made the map about 50% opacity so it would be lighter. Refer to online tutorials to work with layers within your graphics program of choice.

Once your cover is complete, remove the guide boxes and barcode box and save to pdf with the highest quality. Make sure all fonts used are embedded.

Illustration Covers

If you are creating a children's book, you can often use one of the illustrations within the book as a cover image. Just make sure you have room for the text and book description. So choose an illustration that is not too busy.

In the following example, I acquired pizza illustrations from pixabay.com and placed them on the back and front.

You may have to hire an illustrator to create the look you're after. I've created very detailed three-dimensional scenes using high-end 3D programs. Here is one of them.

Again, once your cover is complete, remove the guide boxes and barcode box and save to pdf with the highest quality. Make sure all fonts used are embedded.

Other Cover Examples

The following cover was created using a photo from pixabay.com inserted and cropped for the front cover. For the back cover, I matched the wall color behind the chairs. I created a large rectangle (1500 x 2500 pixels) with graduated color (light top to dark bottom) in Paint Shop Pro and layered a clock onto it. If the images are not rectangular, search for transparent images (.png) so they blend onto the background without showing edges.

For this cover, I made a red rectangle up top and blue for the bottom. I inserted an image of a bald eagle, then placed a photo on the back with the white border into the red.

Amazon Cover Creator

If you are hard-pressed in designing a cover for your book, you can always use Amazon's Cover Creator. You can access it on the KDP platform discussed in the next chapter. It can be used for both print and Kindle books. You'll find it on the Paperback and Kindle ebook Content pages. Templates are provided for you to customize. I prefer creating my own book covers for more flexibility.

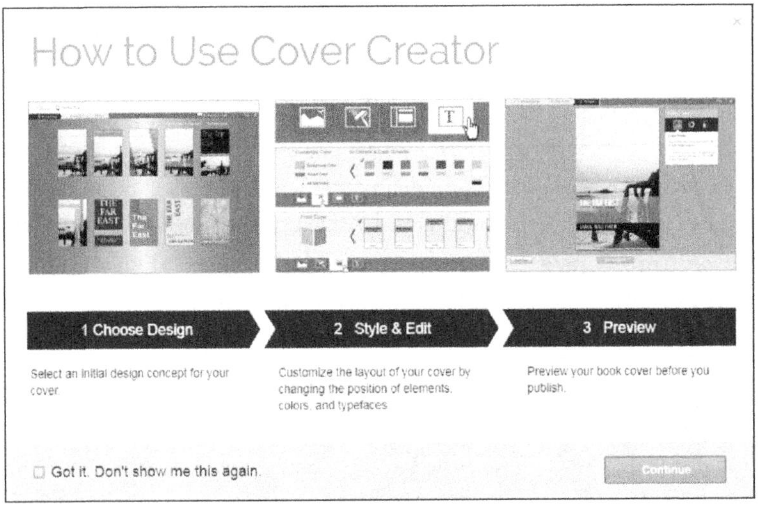

PUBLISHING YOUR BOOK

Overview

Once you have completed your book's interior and cover, you will have two pdf files. These are what you will load onto Amazon's Kindle Direct Publishing (KDP) platform.

ISBN

As stated earlier, you will need to purchase an ISBN number from myidentifiers.com, or you can use a free one from Amazon. It doesn't mean Amazon will own the copyright to your book. It simply means that you will have it printed only through them. If you want the option of having your book printed elsewhere, buy your own ISBN numbers. Once you get your ISBN number, place it on the copyright page as shown earlier, then recreate your book's interior pdf file.

KDP Account

To create your own KDP book publishing account, sign up at http://kdp.amazon.com. Make sure you fill out all tax and payment information so you can receive monthly royalties. Money will be directly deposited into your bank if you elect that option.

You can also order your own book copies at cost from the KDP platform to sell on your own. Cost per book does not vary by quantity, but I suggest that you order at least 20 copies after you approve your physical proof so shipping and handling charges per copy are lower.

Book Setup

To create a new book, click on Bookshelf up top after you log in. Then click on the + for Paperback.

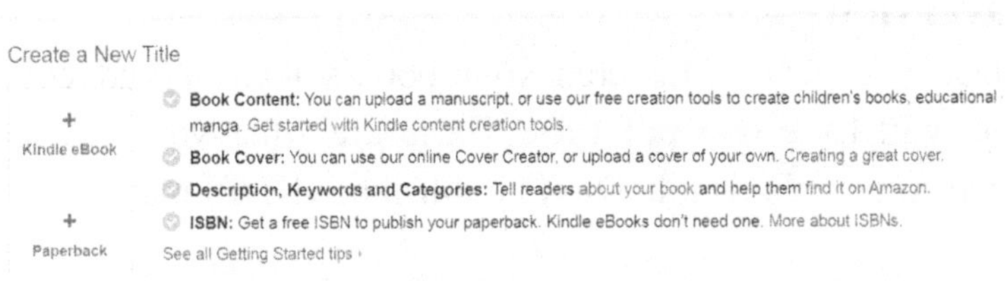

A window will display with the three pages you need to fill out to get your book up on Amazon.

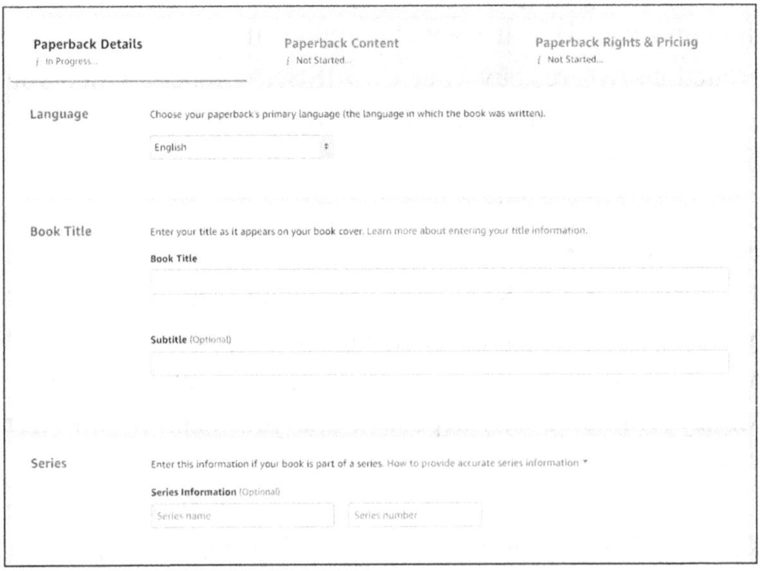

Paperback Details

Here you will enter the title of the book, author name, book description, etc. For my book description, I usually copy exactly what I placed as the description on the back of the book. To force paragraph breaks, type <p><p>.

Make sure you choose the proper categories for your book. It helps to search on Amazon.com to see how similar books are categorized. You also want to be specific with your keywords. If a keyword is already in the book title or subtitle, you do not need to make it a keyword. You can enter up to seven keywords.

Paperback Content

This is where you will enter your ISBN number and load your pdf files. If you already have your own ISBN number, enter it and the imprint name, which is the imprint or company name you registered your ISBNs under on myidentifiers.com. This has to match or they will not accept your book. If you want to have Amazon assign you a free ISBN, make sure you go back and enter it on the copyright page and recreate your interior pdf file before loading it here.

Enter your interior paper type, trim size, bleed settings, and cover finish. I suggest glossy on most books to make the colors pop. Next, load both your manuscript and cover pdf files. Once they have been successfully uploaded and processed, click on Launch Previewer. This will display a digital proof of your book that you can page through and check. Read the left column to see if there are any errors you need to fix.

The outside dotted line is the cut line on the cover, and the inside line is the safety line, meaning all text needs to be inside that. You can also see where the barcode will be printed and if it interferes with your artwork or text.

Page through the entire book and make sure all text is inside the guidelines. If you are satisfied with how everything looks and there are no errors, click Approve. The system will show you what your cost per book will be at the bottom before you click Save and Continue.

Paperback Rights & Pricing

In this section you will want to select All territories and enter your paperback price. The system will calculate the royalties you will make when sold on the worldwide Amazon sites. Choose a reasonable price; you can always change it later. See what similar books are priced on Amazon. Try a lower price first, as long as you are satisfied with the royalties.

Expanded distribution will put your book into more areas, and from my understanding, will make the book available to bookstores like Barnes and Noble *if someone requests it.* Royalties are much lower for that, though.

Click on order proof copies at the bottom to receive a few copies in the mail. It can take a week or so to receive them. Make any changes if you are not satisfied. Once you approve the physical proof, click Publish at the bottom of the Paperback Rights & Pricing page.

In about 24 hours after you approve your book, you can check back to see if there are any errors. Check your email to see what they are and fix them. If you see Live next to the book on your KDP Bookshelf page, that means that everything is okay. Search Amazon and find its detail page for buyers. Share the link with others.

Order Author Copies

You can also order your own copies at cost from the KDP platform. Click on Bookshelf to see all your books. To the far right of the screen along your paperback title you will see three dots (...). Click on that to reveal a menu and select Author copies. Put them in your shopping cart and check out. Again, I suggest ordering at least 20 copies to keep the shipping and handling cost per book low.

KINDLE PUBLISHING

Overview

Once you have approved the text and formatting of your print book, you can now create a Kindle ebook version. To do this, save your print Word document as a different file name. I usually put the word kindle in the name. For example, PoetryPizzaBook is the file name for the print version and PoetryPizzaKindle for the Kindle version.

Formatting

A Kindle version of a print book is basically a stripped-down version. You will want to do the following:

1. Remove all header and footer text.
2. Replace all section breaks with manual page breaks.
3. Remove drop caps and replace with normal text.
4. Remove page numbers from Table of Content.
5. Link Table of Contents to chapters.
6. Convert all Hyperlinks.

Remove headers and footers

Double-click in your headers and footers. Clear out both header text and page numbers at the bottom. Check to make sure all headers and footers are blank throughout the entire document. If not, go to each section and remove them.

Replace section breaks with page breaks

Click on Home-Replace-More and place your cursor in the Find what field. Click on Special. Choose Section Break from the pop-up list.

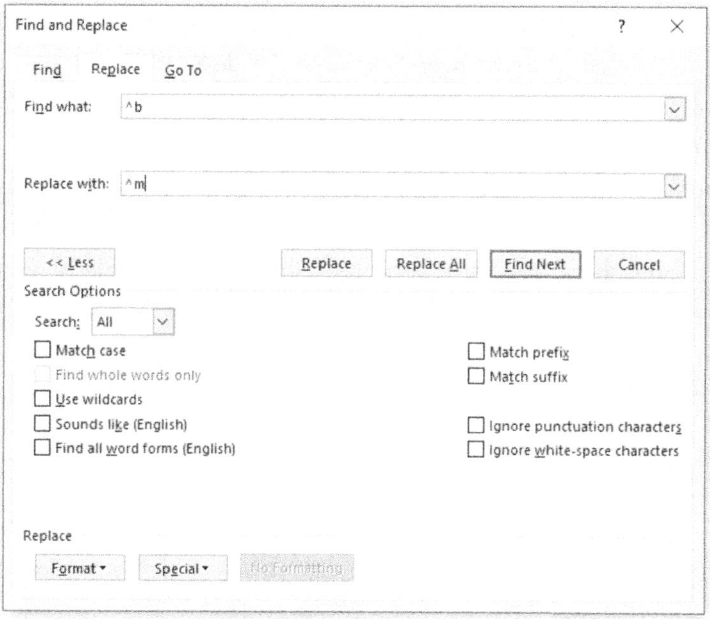

Next, place your cursor in the Replace with field and click on Special. Choose Manual Page Break from the pop-up list. You should see ^b in the Find what field and ^m in the Replace with field. Click on Replace All.

Remove Drop Caps

If you have converted the first letter of a paragraph into a drop cap, you will want to remove that and type back in the first character. This is because most Kindle devices and apps do not recognize drop caps. Another stylistic option would be capitalizing the first few words of the first paragraph in a chapter, if desired.

> Joe and Buddy returned to their car on the side of the road. The passenger door was still wide open.

> JOE AND BUDDY returned to their car on the side of the road. The passenger door was still wide open.

Table of Contents

You will want the table of contents for your ebook to be just links to the chapters and subheadings within your document. Page numbers are not required for Kindle. Delete your current table of contents and recreate it. Uncheck Show page numbers and check Use hyperlinks instead of page numbers.

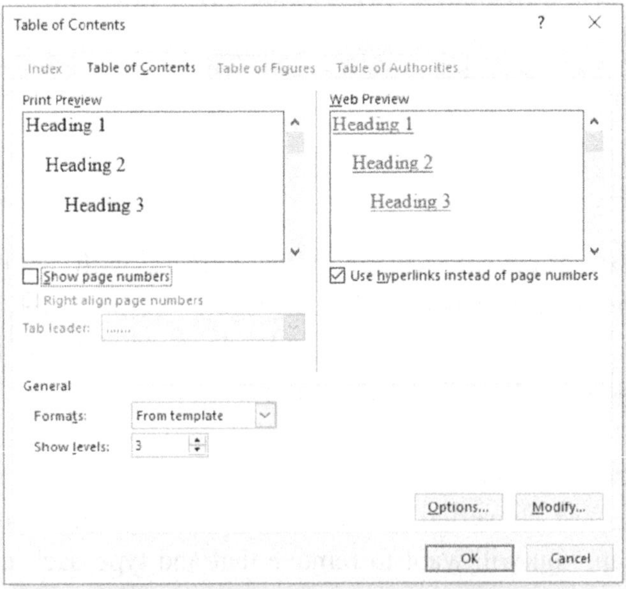

This is how it looks for this book.

TABLE OF CONTENTS

Convert URLs to Hyperlinks

Finally, you will want to convert any existing URLs and email addresses in your book to clickable links. Highlight the text and choose Insert-Hyperlink.

File Cleanup

On the copyright page where you have your ISBN number for the print version, I usually type PRINT ISBNs above the print ISBNs. That will let the reader know that there is also a print version of the ebook available. You are not required to have an ISBN number for the Kindle version of your book, so don't waste one.

Go through your document and make sure there are no odd formatting errors that came up in your step-by-step conversion. You will want to remove any blank pages. If you purposely used a page break within a chapter to force text or images to the next page, you will want to remove that page break and just keep one paragraph return.

Kindle Fonts

Kindle ebooks have a limited font selection. So I suggest making the chapter headings Arial and body text Times New Roman. Or make them both Times New Roman with larger bold chapter headings.

If you are adamant about having a certain font style, for instance, on your interior title page, you can always turn it into a graphic image. Highlight the text, choose Home-Cut and then Paste Special-Picture (jpg).

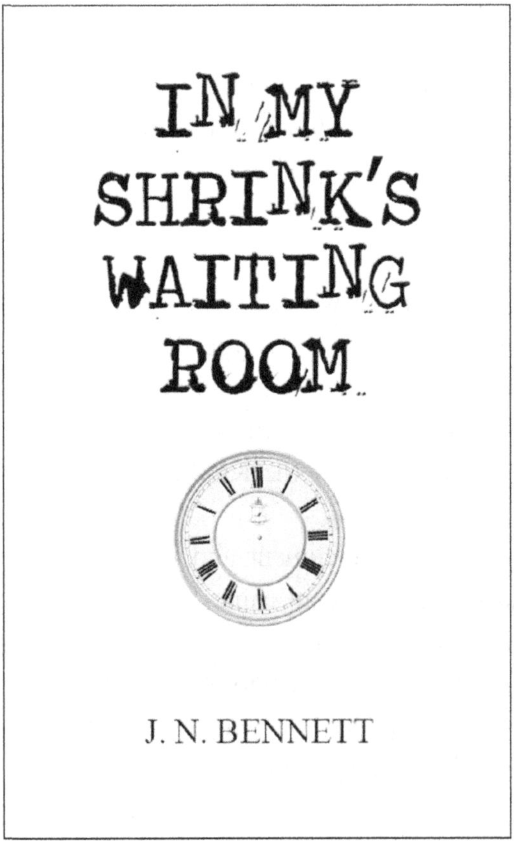

Kindle Cover

Kindle requires that you load a .tif or .jpg image of the front cover. I do this by opening the print cover in Adobe Reader. Zoom to 200%. Then click on Edit-Take a Snapshot. Create a box of any size. Click OK.

Select Edit-Select All and Edit-Copy to copy the entire cover. Then in a graphics program like Paint Shop Pro, select Edit-Paste-As New Image. Now select just the front cover and choose Image-Crop to Selection. Save the front cover as an uncompressed RGB .tif file.

Publishing

Once you are satisfied with your Word Kindle document and your cover image, you are ready to upload them to the KDP platform. Go to your Bookshelf and click on + Create Kindle ebook in the same row as your print book.

Most of the information will already be filled out for the Kindle ebook Details page. Check to make sure. Click Save and Continue.

Loading Files

On the following page, you will load your Kindle Word file under Manuscript and your cover image under Kindle ebook Cover. Make sure you check Upload a cover you already have.

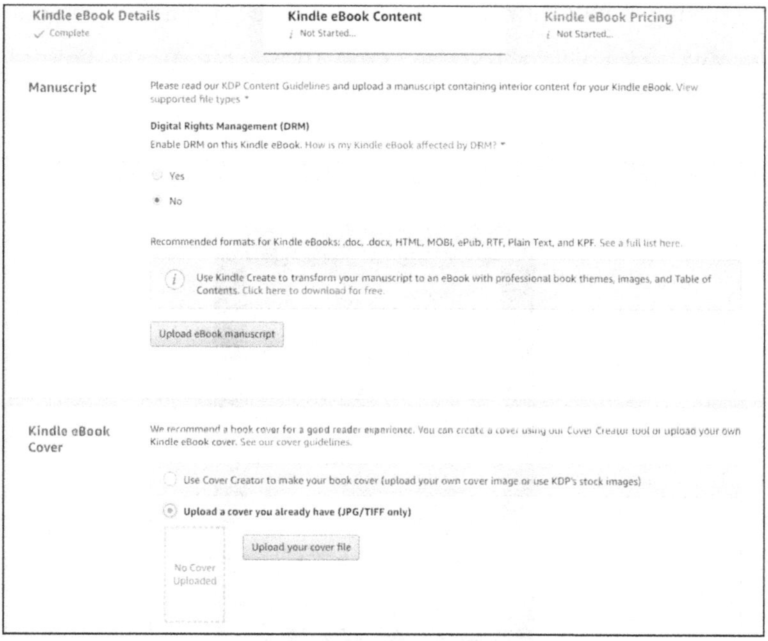

Previewing Ebook

Once both files are loaded, you will want to test to see how your ebook will look on various devices: Kindle, tablet, smartphone, etc. There are several ways to do this. You can click on Launch Previewer, or download a mobi file and view it on your Kindle or Previewer program. I like to try all ways since the online previewer is not always that accurate.

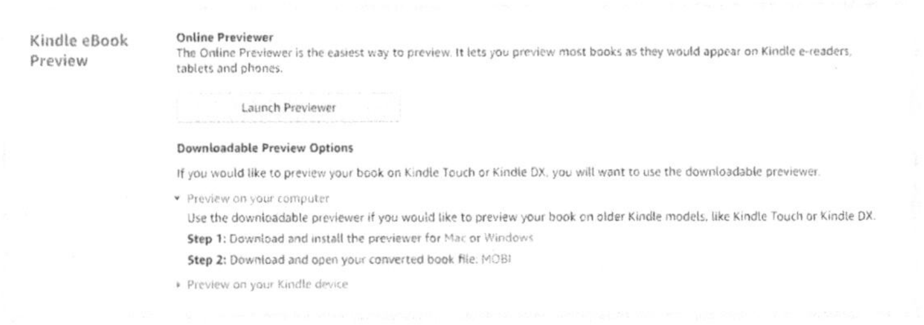

Using Launch Previewer, you will see a window similar to this. You can select the type of device you'd like to preview the book on using the top-right pulldown.

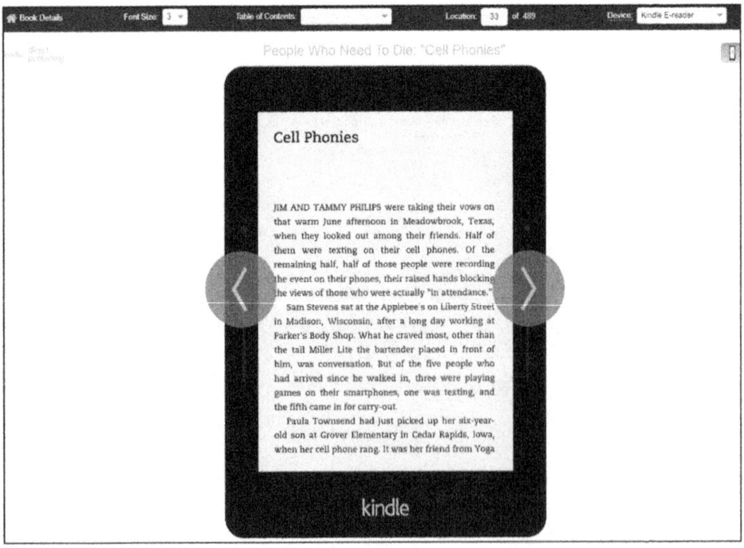

Page through the book by hovering your mouse on the sides of the virtual device and clicking the arrows. Once you have paged through every page, click on Book Details in the top-left corner to return to the Kindle eBook Content page. There you can download and install the Kindle Previewer application and the mobi file.

Open the mobi ebook file in the computer Kindle Previewer. It may take some time to load. You will get a screen similar to this:

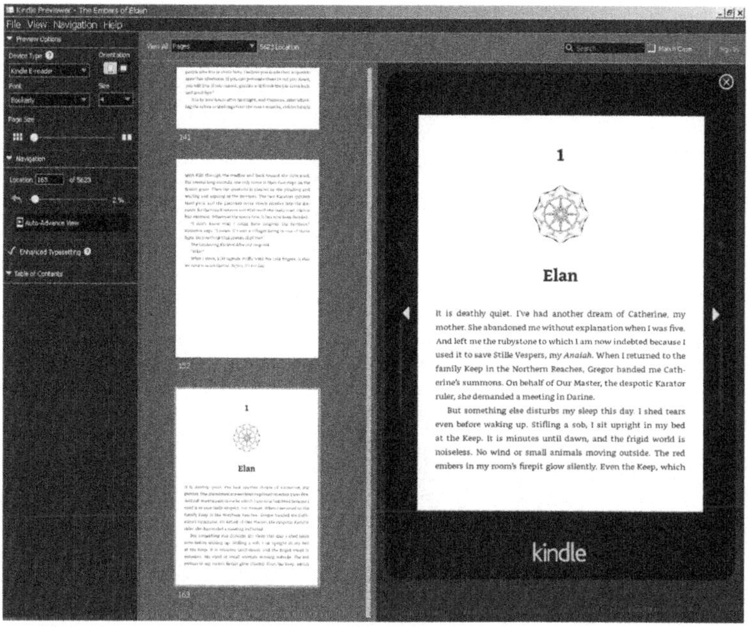

You can select the Device Type on the top left of the screen. Page through the book using the arrow keys.

There is yet a third way to preview your Kindle book. If you own a Kindle device, there is an email address associated with it that should end in @kindle.com. Go to Settings on your Kindle device and page through to find out what your device email address is. Now email your .mobi file to that email address with no subject. Your book will appear in your list momentarily. Now you can preview your book on your own device. If you need to make changes to your Kindle Word document, do so and preview it until it looks correct.

Pricing Ebook

Once you are satisfied with how your ebook looks, click Save and Continue. Choose All territories and enter your selling price. To receive 70% royalties, you will have to price your book between $2.99 and $9.99.

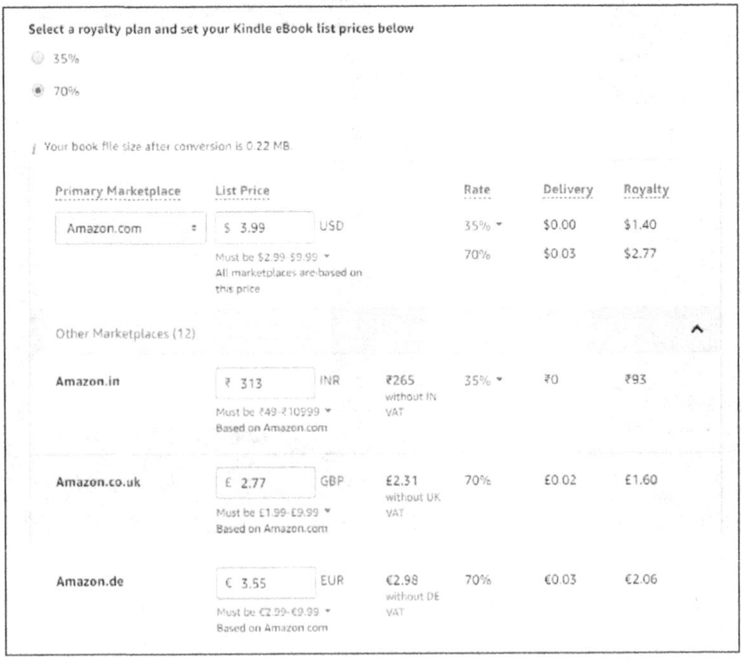

A good start would be somewhere in the middle. Allow for Lending and click on Publish Your Kindle ebook.

SELLING YOUR BOOK

Overview

I've added this chapter because I've learned a lot about marketing and selling books over the past few years. It takes *a lot* of effort to get your books into the hands of readers. But think of it this way: if you took months or even years to write a book, you should expect to spend the same amount of time marketing it. You can still write other books, but always keep promoting your previous ones. You never know what will make things take off. Here are some ways to get the word out.

Word of Mouth

The best form of marketing is word-of-mouth. Tell your friends and family and co-workers. Some will buy, some will not. I've learned that the people close to you often don't want to see you as an author, but don't let that stop you from getting a few sales. And don't let it get you down if they show no interest. The idea is to start finding your audience. Get 10 people hooked on everything you write, and soon that will increase to 20 or more. Whenever someone buys your book, ask them to take a picture of them with your book and post it on social media. We'll get to the benefits and limitations of social media in a bit.

Book Signings

There are many avenues for you to sign your books in person at little to no cost. Pair up with mom-and-pop shops and ask if you can be a guest author for the day. Try coffeehouses, independent bookstores, craft and holiday shows—any place where you can appropriately reach your audience and set up a small table. You'll want to have a large 18" x 24" poster foam-core mounted and laminated to stand out and attract people to come over. Make sure people are aware of when and where you'll be signing before the event through flyers and social media.

You mustn't be shy at book signings. Engage anyone who walks by in conversation. I like to ask, "Do you like to read? I have some books I've written that may interest you." Or simply, "How is your day going today?" Often times people need a little coaxing to get over their *own* shyness about approaching strangers. Be kind, and reel them in.

When they are at your table, hand them your book so they are forced to hold it. Let them read the back cover. Tell them about the book while they have it in hand. Many purchases are spur of the moment. Getting it in their hands is one step away from them owning it. If they do whip out cash or a credit card, make sure you can provide change and have an app on your phone, like Square, that can take credit card payments.

You may want to give out goodies like bookmarks and cards. If someone asks for your card, that is usually a clue that they are not going to buy right then, and probably never will. But it doesn't hurt to hand them something to remember you by. Make sure your email address and website are on it. Oh, you don't have a website yet? You better create one. Let's talk about that.

Author Website/Blog

Every author needs some kind of online presence. That could be a website/blog, a dedicated Facebook author page, a Twitter account, etc. I've created blogs and websites using Google's Blogger platform, which is free hosting. You can also try WordPress, though they charge for advanced features.

You'll want to post updates on your blog at least once a week. That could include snippets from your books, or other projects you are working on. Share the blog page links on Facebook and Twitter so anyone who clicks on them will be directed back to your website. Once there, they can discover everything about you and maybe even buy your books. Make sure you provide pictures of your books and links to their order pages on Amazon.

If you need a website or blog and don't want to create it yourself, contact me at vic@victorrook.com and I'll set one up for you.

Facebook Debugger

I'm going to let you in on a little secret. Sometimes when you share web posts on Facebook, they won't always appear as you want them to. The goal is to get an image and the first few lines of text from your blog post within the share. To do this, you need to make sure you have text in your blog post *before* any photos, like an introductory paragraph. And the photo you want to share needs to be the largest photo within the post. That's how Facebook's algorithm creates a preview.

Luckily, there's a tool called Facebook Debugger that will let you see how Facebook will share your post. Go to https://developers.facebook.com/tools/debug/sharing/ and paste in your blog post or web page URL. Click Debug, Fetch new information, and then Scrape Again.

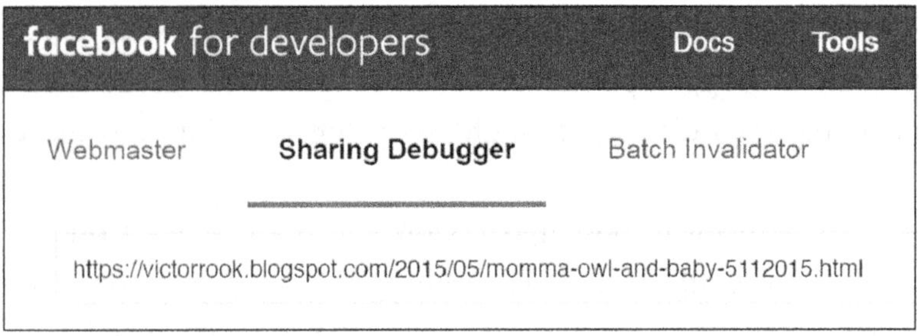

Not only will it show you how your post will appear when you share it on Facebook, put it will also give you information on open graph (og) properties that you might want to include as meta tags within your shared page. But that's something to be discussed in another book.

Fetched URL https://victorrook.blogspot.com/2014/12/sold-out-book-signing-at-2nd-charles.html

Canonical URL http://victorrook.blogspot.com/2014/12/sold-out-book-signing-at-2nd-charles.html
18 likes, shares and comments (More Info)

Redirect Path Input URL → https://victorrook.blogspot.com/2014/12/sold-out-book-signing-at-2nd-charles.html
og:url Meta Tag → http://victorrook.blogspot.com/2014/12/sold-out-book-signing-at-2nd-charles.html

Link Preview

VICTORROOK.BLOGSPOT.COM
SOLD OUT! Book Signing at 2nd & Charles
Manager Kim from 2nd & Charles stopped by for a photo op with the few...

Social Media

This could be a book on its own. Aside from sharing your books on Facebook and your own website, you can also reach people via other online sites. Ask if you can be a guest blogger on someone else's blog, or have them review your book. Put your books up on review sites like goodreads.com. Enter writing contests for your book where the fee is minimal and the exposure is great. Join Facebook groups that align with your book's topic and mention it. Just don't overdo solicitation. Sometimes it's better to mention your book in the comments section of someone else's post. There are countless ways to tell people about your book online.

News Media

As soon as your book is available for purchase, start contacting the local newspapers. Write a press release. See if you can find someone who has an "in" with the writers that you can talk to in person. Make sure you share every bit of publicity you get on Facebook, Twitter, and your blog.

Writers Clubs

If you are not already involved in a local writing group, check around and find one. They serve as an invaluable resource for connecting with others and learning about different events. You'll become friends with various authors who can tell you how they've been successful (or unsuccessful) in reaching their target audiences. If anything, they can give you emotional support.

Pay it Forward

Being an author that actually sells books is not an easy task. But you mustn't give up. Even if you only sell five in the first month. Five is better than none. My advice is to always look for avenues where you can connect with people face to face. You are not only selling your book, but yourself. Once people feel connected to you, they are more apt to buy. You can do this online as well by responding to others in a friendly manner. Showing interest in others' work is a great way of establishing a good rapport. People like to share things with others who help them. So make a point of reaching out beyond yourself.

OTHER WRITING TOOLS

Scrivener

Scrivener allows you to write and organize your document chapters through index cards that you can post and rearrange on a virtual corkboard. It also allows you to keep track of all your research material. You can export your final document to pdf, ebook, and other file types. Download a free trial of the program at https://www.literatureandlatte.com.

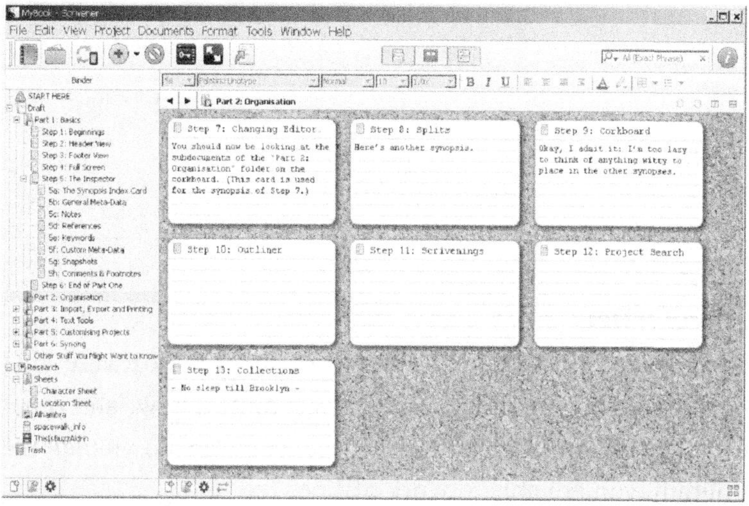

Google Docs

Google Docs allows you to create, edit, format, and share documents online from any location. You can add images, hyperlinks, tables, headers, footers, and more. Because files are saved in the cloud, you can allow access to others to edit or proof them. At any time you can download what you've written in several formats, including pdf and MS-Word. Choose File-Download. Once you have a Google account, you can access Google Docs at https://docs.google.com.

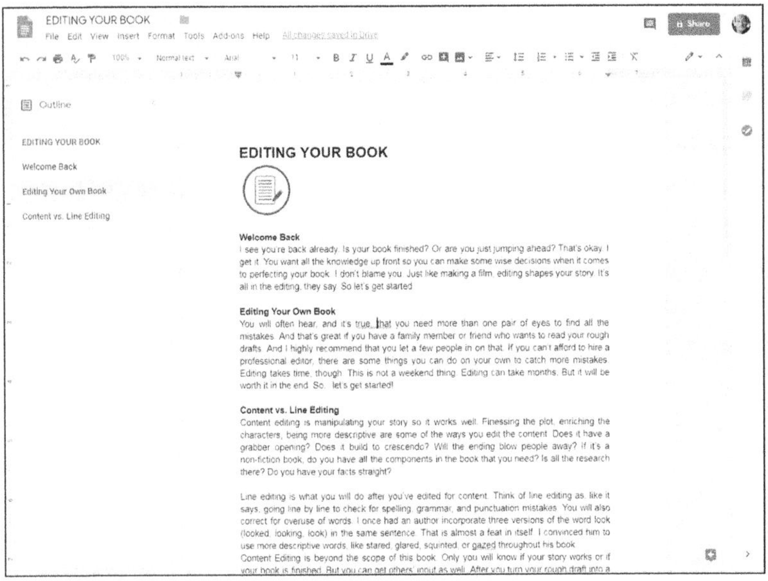

LibreOffice

Don't have MS-Office? LibreOffice is free software that includes Writer, Impress (like PowerPoint), Draw, and other programs within the suite. Because you can download the program, you are able to work offline.

The Writer interface is very similar to older versions of MS-Word, which I prefer. You have your File, Edit, Insert, Format, and Tools menus for easy access to formatting and page setup. You can also import existing Word documents, and Export to Word. You can even export to pdf and epub. Download at http://libreoffice.org.

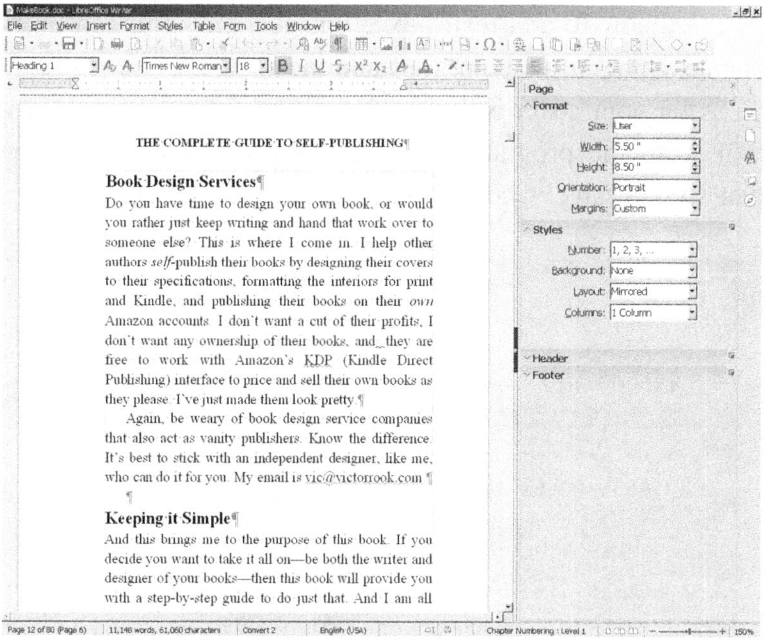

The one drawback with Writer is creating the separate headers and footers for each chapter. The Insert-Section command is not the same as the Section Break command in MS-Word. To create a new chapter with different first page, left page, and right page headers, you must go to Style-Manage Styles, and click on the Page Styles icon. You need to keep duplicating the first chapter style after you have it correctly set up and name the new styles Chapter 2, Chapter 3, etc. It's very complicated and too cumbersome.

Because ebooks do not require headers or footers, consider using Writer to create Kindle versions with the epub export. Choose Export As-Export Directly as EPUB.

Impress, which is LibreOffice's presentation program, allowed me to design covers just as I do in PowerPoint. Some of the menu items are in a different place, so take time to get to know how to add text, boxes, images, etc. You can even open existing PowerPoint files into the program.

After your cover is designed, you can export it directly to PDF with the program's own built-in pdf generator. Now that's Impressive! Choose Export As-Directly to PDF.

EverNote

Evernote is a mobile app for note taking. Tap in your ideas, outlines, research notes, etc. Search your phone's app store to download to your phone.

Reedsy

How about an entire online book writing, formatting, and publishing tool that creates both print-ready pdfs and ebook files? That's what Reedsy was designed to do. And, it's free.

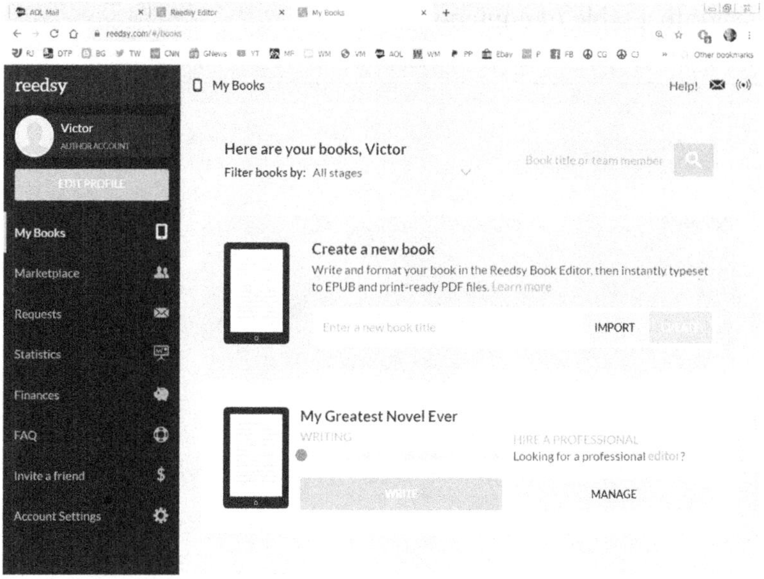

After you create your login, you can import existing text or start a new document. As you type, the online writer will automatically indent the first line of subsequent paragraphs. You can format text along the way simply by highlighting it. Your text will be saved to the cloud automatically.

The left panel allows you to move chapters around and access other tools. You can also have the writer automatically generate a copyright page by answering a few questions. You'll have to pre-purchase an ISBN number. It will also generate a table of contents.

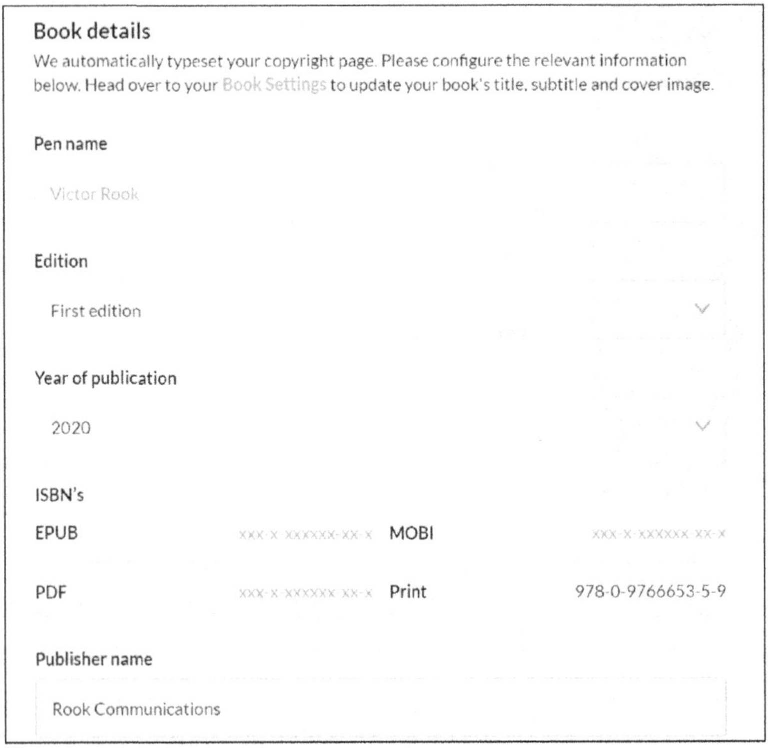

You *will* see squiggly lines under words that might be misspelled when you write your book, but there is no grammar or punctuation checker. Reedsy offers those services at a cost, which is probably how they make their money. Still, it's a nice interface to put a book together if you don't want to take the time to format heading styles and headers and footers on your own as you would need to do in MS-Word.

After your book is complete, you can export it by clicking on the Export down arrow. You will have to upload your own book cover image under Book Settings. There is no cover designer at this time.

If you choose PDF, you have the option of four book trim sizes (Amazon will not print the Pocket size) and currently three formatting templates.

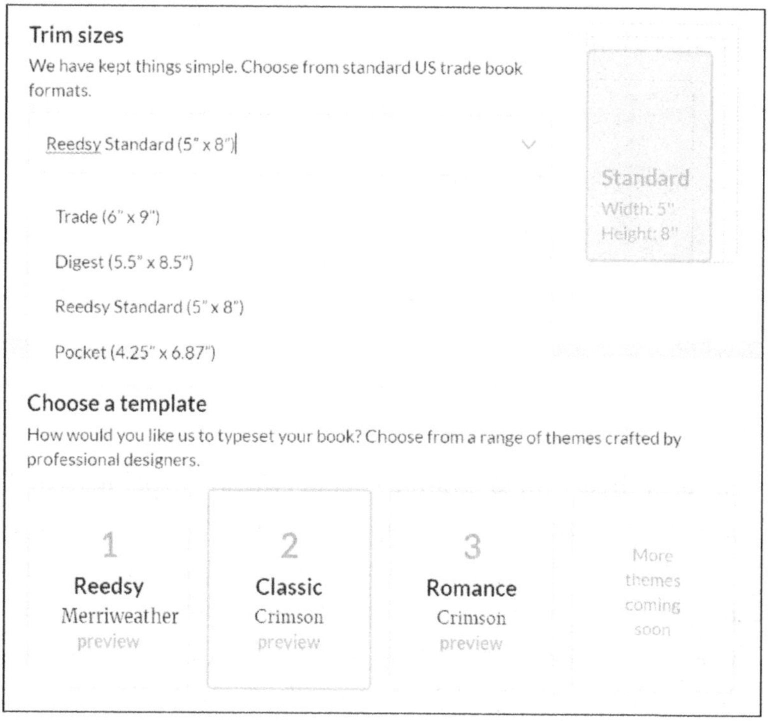

Once everything is selected, click on Export Book and wait for an email to download the pdf. You can also have the book exported in epub and mobi formats. http://reedsy.com

Grammarly

Grammarly is a desktop app and a browser extension for Chrome that will check for spelling, punctuation, and grammar errors. It also checks for things like wordiness and plagiarism. Again, not all grammar checkers are foolproof. Download at http://grammarly.com.

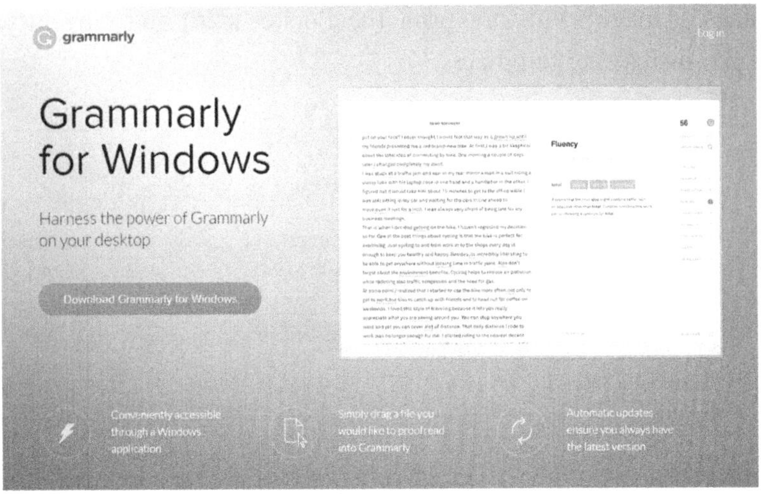

Virtual Writing Tutor

This is a free online grammar, punctuation, spelling, and vocabulary checker. Simply copy and paste text into the large box on the main page and choose which criteria you'd like to examine. Non-members can paste 500 words at a time. Members can paste 3000. Be sure to turn off your ad blocker before you create a login. You can still choose no ads.

I also like the text-to-speech function. By clicking on the text-to-speech speaker icon below the box, you can have a voice read back what you've written. I find this very helpful in catching mistakes, like missing words. Another icon allows you to save the recording as a .mp3 file. It's a treat to hear a voice read your own work to you. Albeit, it *is* a computer-generated voice, but it's actually not that bad. Go to http://virtualwritingtutor.com to access the interface.

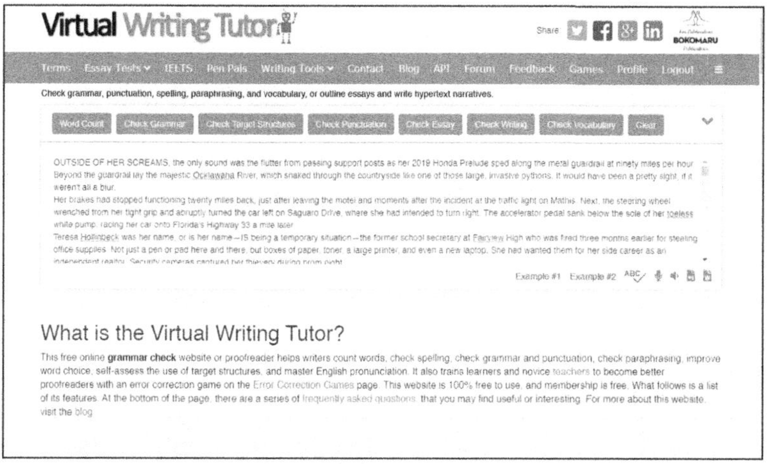

In Conclusion

There are tons of tools available on the web to help with all facets of writing, editing, and formatting. Search Youtube for videos if you need visual instructions. Chances are if you're having a problem somewhere along the line, someone else has already come up with a solution and posted a video on it. Or written an informative blog post. The answers, as always, are at your fingertips.

I must leave you now. Let me know if this book has been helpful to you and please rate it on Amazon. And if you are looking for assistance at a reasonable cost, feel free to contact me at vic@victorrook.com.

Victor Rook

ACKNOWLEDGMENTS

The following books were featured in this publication:

1. *Young Heroes of the Lost Lake* by Alan Bonsall
2. *The Pigtail Princess* by Tom Basham
3. *Time to Go* by David Major
4. *I Closed Too Many Eyes* by Paul Arneson
5. *Dead Fish* by Deno Seder
6. *A Family of One* by Kenneth M. Brenneman
7. *In My Shrink's Waiting Room* by J. N. Bennett
8. *Poetry Schmoetry* by J. N. Bennett
9. *The Decline of the American Experiment* by Gregory K. Petty
10. *The Memory Witch* by T. R. Dillon
11. *Poetry Pizza* by Victor Rook
12. *People Who Need to Die* by Victor Rook

All books can be ordered on Amazon.com.

NOTES

Made in the USA
Monee, IL
04 November 2026

67377481R00056